BANI RAWAL

Debate Like a Champion: The Public Forum Edition

*How Any Middle Schooler Can Learn Public Forum,
Speak with Confidence, and Win — From a Student
Who Did It*

First edition

ISBN: 979-8-9937593-0-2

This book was professionally typeset on Reedsy.
Find out more at reedsy.com

To every student who ever felt afraid to speak — this book is for you.

Contents

Acknowledgments

Thank you to my family for believing in me, to my teachers for encouraging my voice, and to my fellow debaters and students who have inspired me to teach, learn, and grow through every round. Your support, guidance, and encouragement made this book possible. I am grateful for every lesson, every challenge, and every breakthrough that shaped my debate journey.

I

Part One

This part briefly highlights how I essentially started my debate career as well as what made debate more enjoyable beyond the competitive aspect of it. Debate is forever going to be an element that I admire and honestly, you need to enjoy yourself while being out there competing because that is what is going to end up being your biggest motivators when you're in that random classroom debating.

1

The Spark

U p until 6th grade, I remember my parents always comparing me to my friends in terms of achievements.

"See, Kaylee got an award for being good at math! She probably has so many awards to decorate her entire house."

And, "Mark is so good at swimming that he got like thirty awards for it. See! Here!"

I didn't really do anything. I was kind of taking it easy in life because I didn't really find anything too interesting. I didn't do any sports or extracurriculars and didn't do much at home either.

I thought sports were very aggressive and not really accessible to me in my apartment in the city, which wasn't very close to any parks. At home, I liked to watch cartoons or play Roblox with my brother. I liked to sleep. That was my talent — one I should've won awards for.

But eventually, when I saw that my school, The Anderson School on the Upper West Side of Manhattan, NYC, had a lot to offer, I wondered what I was really good at. My parents wanted me to win something — do something with my life — so I was going to do just that. I just had to find the right thing.

Eventually, I did.

It wasn't easy. Despite being the rambunctious and extroverted person I was then, I was scared of the judgement that came with being on any of my school's clubs or teams. I wasn't scared of the judgement of my own classmates, the ones I had spent so much time with since kindergarten.

I was scared of the judgement of the upperclassmen.

Yes, the upperclassmen who ran down the halls even though they were told not to. The upperclassmen who always walked around in their cliques, probably laughing about how they were twice my height.

How frightening.

In 5th grade, I had always been delighted by the idea of being on my school's debate team. I was really loud when I was younger. I always raised my hand if my teacher was talking about something and brought up something slightly irrelevant but still interesting. I always joked around with my classmates during work time, but I managed to get all my work done within ten minutes — and with full marks.

Joining the debate club would allow me to talk as much as I wanted *and* be awarded for it! What a beautiful way to spend my time. I was good at those random persuasive essays my ELA teacher used to assign, and I was always dramatic enough to my parents to be a star in a movie.

What talents did I not possess to be a stellar debater? My ego was at its peak, and debate was only going to ignite its flames further.

So when 6th grade began and I sat in my social studies classroom, looking up at my teachers, I was *bubbly.* My fingers drummed against the table in exhilaration as I listened to whatever my debate coaches, Mr. Mucha and Mr. Fox, had to say.

Then came the golden words: "upcoming debate tournament at Columbia University in December 2022."

My ears perked up. I knew at this point that my parents would be extremely impressed with me if I competed there. I *craved* my parents' attention — I wanted them to acknowledge how amazing I was at everything. But also, this was my chance to finally compete at my dream university. I knew I wanted to pursue law ever since my 5th grade field trip to a courthouse and doing a mock trial.

When the announcement was over, I eagerly walked around the room, asking everyone if they wanted to be my partner.

To my disappointment, nobody wanted to be my partner. They said they only came to debate club to use the iPads to play games or were too shy to actually compete.

I felt a pit in my stomach. I was being stopped by something I didn't think would ever be a problem.

I sat in my seat, despair filling my face. As I slumped in my chair, the girl next to me — the first one I had asked — said that maybe she could ask her parents if she could compete.

Glee filled my eyes. I *finally* had a partner! I could finally compete at the tournament that I thought was a far-fetched dream or goal.

After I finally had a set partner, I began to prepare for the tournament like a maniac. I finished nearly the entire case within three days (which I learned in the far future to NEVER do) and printed out a copy to show my debate coaches. I asked them to proofread it and give me feedback. Their feedback was something I was extremely reliant on because nobody really taught me how to write a case except for the basic structure of having the reason, evidence, and impact.

"Bani, I think you have too many arguments... all of your arguments are around five sentences, and I think you need to go deeper," Mr. Mucha told me. "I recommend you start with two arguments since it's your first tournament."

I hummed in reply. I usually absolutely hated it when teachers told me that I wrote too much and that I needed to shorten what I wrote. I always felt like they didn't value all the hard work I put into their assignments. I loved writing a lot because I was a yapper, and writing let me express everything I wanted to without annoying my friends so much (I never annoy my friends — they love me).

But I soon realized that my coaches weren't actually telling me to delete what I had written. They simply wanted me to choose two arguments to yap about and then weave in what the spare arguments were about into the main two. This covered several burdens of mine as a casewriter: having arguments that were well structured and having arguments that anticipated potential refutations from the opponent.

My coaches definitely played a fundamental part in my debate journey. Whenever I was at a debate tournament, my opponents always said they had really strict coaches who honestly didn't coach them at all. Those coaches wrote their cases for them and did all the research for them. That couldn't possibly help a debater really immerse themselves in the topic they were debating, and they probably had the same arguments as the rest of their team.

Our coaches helped us grow by letting us just learn on our own. They pushed me out there to really understand how to understand debate — my second tournament showing more brilliant results than the first proved this exactly!

My coaches didn't criticize the way we debated either. Instead, they just gave us feedback. You might think that this is the bare minimum, but after debate rounds where my opponents' coach was watching, I noticed that coaches often deprecated their debaters and compared them to famous speakers. My coaches just let us go with the flow.

I think I was also able to create an amazing bond with both of my coaches by being in their classes for two years each for social studies — their classes themselves giving me material to bring up in crossfire or use as a refutation to an argument. I always loved being able to see them throughout the day.

I knew one of my coaches, Mr. Fox, since I was in second grade, as I always snuck down to his classroom during lunch to play with his class fish, "Alexander Swamilton." I remember his welcoming smile every time, despite knowing an elementary schooler wasn't really supposed to be wandering the middle school floor hallways.

Mr. Mucha's 5th and 6th grade social studies class was always a delight, with him conforming to the humor of a middle schooler. His class really got me into global history for high school, and I'm always bringing elements from his class into debate (and sometimes using his legendary roasts to crack a laugh). Both of my coaches really did "raise" my debate career, and I'm extremely thankful to them for it.

I had a hard time deciding what arguments to "delete" that night. All of the arguments were written by us, so they had to be perfect, right?

But alas, I had to choose two. Two for each side.

I remember the topic being about a ban on social media or something similar to that. There were many reasons to hate or love social media, and I thought I had to point out every single one; otherwise, the opponent and judge would think I was ignoring a super important factor.

Now, I know that this is quite the opposite of what I have to do when casewriting. I have to accept the fact that not everything can be said about a topic within a three-minute timeframe. I had to accept that there were disadvantages in debate that were meant to exist because that's what made it genuinely challenging.

It's a brutal exercise, trying to identify the two most foundational arguments — the two that, if shattered, would crumble the entire structure. It's not just about removing words; it's about reconceptualizing the entire argument, finding the overarching themes that encompass the smaller supporting points.

I'm searching for that elusive golden thread that ties everything together, allowing me to weave a compelling narrative with just two pillars of persuasion. The pressure is immense, but the challenge is exhilarating — to prove that less truly can be more, even when it feels like I'm leaving so much unsaid.

After a few hours, I finally chose two arguments for each side and felt happy with myself, immediately pressing Command+P to print out another copy to give to my debate coach.

I think on that day, I didn't realize that what I had accomplished could've been done in ten minutes, yet I had spent hours on it. This actually meant a lot, though, because it gave me a personal feeling that I was taking debate seriously and putting my best foot forward in order to do better.

I wasn't going to magically get better, so I counted on the feedback I was getting. Usually, I hated getting feedback because I always thought people were just trying to nitpick whatever I did since I was always "perfect." I didn't like changing things when they were already fully written out. My mindset was that once it was on the paper, it was there forever.

This mindset was also found in my schoolwork. It irritated me immensely when my teachers asked us to submit first drafts and final drafts. I secretly never really did those drafts and just submitted the "final version" both times — with the only change being grammatical edits.

Eventually, while my debate career progressed, my mindset changed along with it. I started really seeing the value in planning things out — essays or not — before actually committing to a final project. It genuinely helps you make something the best it can be. This is a critical life skill, and that was a statement I refused to admit until the last few months of 8th grade.

While I waited for feedback, I worked hard on improving my speaking by reciting the lines over and over again each night. When I discussed the case with my debate coach, he mentioned that he had indeed read what I put together, but said, "I think you should review it on your own. I mean, it's good." He gave me a few suggestions, and I took them happily.

My debate coach was a very chill and laid-back person, so this honestly made me feel a lot more relaxed about the upcoming tournament.

Looking back at the case I wrote, it wasn't the most impressive piece of argumentative writing I've ever put together — not to be too hard on my 6th grade self. But I'll take it as a sign of how much I improved my writing and debating skills.

So, I forgot about the feedback, and I didn't make any further efforts to improve my case. I kind of just let it be and practiced my speaking skills instead.

What I *should* have done was learn how the actual debate works. I was absolutely clueless.

This factor was going to stress me out so much in the first round on tournament day.

But until then, I slept peacefully.

During our first round, I thought both the first and second speaker would say arguments in their speeches. I had a bit of luck when my brain finally processed the fact that the rebuttal speech was just to *refute* —

not to bring up the entire second argument we didn't say.

We only had one argument presented in our constructive speech for our very first round. Wonderful.

I noticed that our competitors had brought a spectator with them — a very annoying one. He kept giggling at what were obviously YouTube Shorts and then showing his friends the videos in the middle of the round.

I was irritated, but I didn't want to lose my cool. Besides, this was my first debate round ever, and I knew the judge was seeing what I was seeing.

My partner gave her speech, and everything after that was a blur. I remember not really being able to hear our opponents, so my summary speech was just summarizing our own arguments and not theirs.

Somehow, we won.

My partner and I linked our hands under the table. We had won our first debate round ever! After that round, we celebrated by sitting in the halls of the Hamilton building and eating a giant family pack of Takis.

The second round was a blur and not very interesting — our opponents didn't talk a lot and mumbled through their speeches, so we won that too.

This was when my ego started kicking in again. We were going to EAT the third round and leave no crumbs.

This round is still one of the funniest debate rounds I have ever experienced.

The opponents gave their constructive speech first, and the second they were done, I knew these girls did not mumble. They didn't giggle with their friends in the background. They were serious. They had EXPERIENCE — the one thing that *we* lacked.

Their coach was watching our round, as well as my father. I remember that their coach had no manners whatsoever for a debate round. She talked through the speeches and gave her team motivational remarks and looks. She gave our team nasty looks as well as some surprisingly respectful ones, with occasional comments such as, "Damn girl, you get that!" and eventually, "This is better than Wednesday and all my telenovelas!"

Eventually, we knew we were being crushed by the team when we couldn't reply to any of the questions during crossfire, and I blanked out through my entire summary speech. But when their coach made one more remark, my partner lost it.

"Can you please STOP talking? It's so disrespectful!" my partner snapped.

The debate coach looked astounded but did not reply. She leaned back in her seat and stayed quiet for the rest of the round.

When the judge announced our first loss ever, I wasn't as crestfallen as I thought I would be because I knew I did poorly that round. I knew this was going to happen at this tournament eventually. I was more annoyed by the fact that the opposing team's coach still had the audacity to say "Good job" with that smile that I *knew* wasn't fake, but I like to say it was.

Ew. Get your positivity out of my face.

After that round was lunch break — pizza in Lerner Hall. Our school huddled around the end of the staircase, as all the other spots were taken. We chatted about our rounds and the silly things that happened over Takis, pizza, and a weird concoction of a Taki dipped in Fanta.

Glorious.

At the end of the day, we finished with a 2−2 win−loss ratio. It wasn't bad for a first tournament, so I was proud of myself. But I was even prouder of my school's team because one partnership of debaters from our school made it into the final round.

I watched the round with intense curiosity as a one-man team (the other partner had complications and couldn't compete) from our school went against two biting high school girls.

The round ended with me believing that the high school girls would win — not because I didn't have faith in us, but because they simply attacked his points so well and spoke so well.

I was astounded when they announced during the award ceremony that *he* had won first place. First!

I was even more astounded when they announced my name for the Outstanding Speaker award for my school. I had actually made an achievement. I had gotten a certificate — a token to show my parents that I truly was capable of winning something in life!

I gloated my award to my proud-looking father who was waiting in the crowd for me.

But I didn't just take away from these rounds that the opponent was annoying and that their coach was annoying and that everything about them was super-duper annoying.

I took their skills.

It sounds a little like a crime, but that's the only way people truly learn. They borrow tips and tricks that they saw their opponents use and then apply them to their next round. This sounds so simple, but it really wasn't. I wrote down the feedback that the judge gave to my opponents and applied it to myself.

This is not only how you become like your opponents — but how you become *better* than them.

Oh, how I love the competitive thrill of everything.

After the overwhelming event, we finally headed home, and I remember that day as one filled with many memories of running around and being foolish on my dream university's campus.

Looking back on the tournaments at Youth for Debate at Columbia University, I think those tournaments were honestly the ones that helped me improve the most as a debater. The judges at Youth for Debate were genuinely interested and experienced in debate since they created the program on their own. This was very different compared to the judges

I've faced in other leagues — parent judges who honestly couldn't care less about debate and were only judging because their child's team needed to fill a judging requirement.

While I think it's admirable for parents to step up and serve leagues in such a critical way, I think something that could make the debate experience a lot more worthwhile for both the judge and the debater is simply giving genuine feedback and trying to fully grasp what's going on in the debate. This feedback will eventually help kids so much that by the next time those parent judges judge a round, the rounds will be much more entertaining to listen to — and much more rewarding to judge.

Honestly, the biggest highlight of all my debate tournaments has been just being able to hang out with my team. I've spent nine years at The Anderson School and practically grew up with all my classmates, and being on a team made me feel closer to people I didn't expect to be close with. It gave me a source of people to rely on if I ever felt stuck in my extracurriculars, and I started to see the value in joining teams, which everybody always seemed to emphasize so much.

2

Looking into the Mirror

Yeah. What was the point of that entire debate tournament? I realized I had amazing speaking potential (obviously), but how did I make our arguments better? Every judge and coach told me that was the critical aspect of debate. I had to actually learn how to make my arguments better instead of remaining stagnant.

It didn't take me long to figure out that this was generally the point of debate — to perfect yourself every single time and try to attain the unattainable: being completely perfect. It was really rubbed in my face by everyone in their feedback and speaking.

I had to take what I learned from the first tournament at Youth for Debate at Columbia University and apply it to the next, at a different league — the New York City Urban Debate League. I had learned quite a lot. It was honestly impossible to do well in the first tournament considering the fact that I knew nothing about how a debate round was actually structured before entering it. It was hard to admit that I had done something wrong, but debate humbled me in a way that nothing else really could have.

After some embarrassing rounds where I couldn't even speak during crossfire, I realized that I needed to improve so I wouldn't be embarrassed again. This was, at first, one of my biggest motivators to do better, if I'm being completely honest. But during final rounds, I noticed that nobody kept quiet — they were quick on their feet. That was a skill I needed, along with many others.

I learned that I needed to structure my arguments in a way that fit the time constraints perfectly. I learned from listening to feedback that the judges gave to my opponents that even having leftover time was bad. I also learned that even though I was the first speaker, I needed to pay attention to what my opponent was saying and not leave that entire responsibility to my partner, even though they delivered the rebuttal speech.

The list of things I learned was endless, but I needed to figure out how to apply them not only in the casewriting part, but also unconsciously in the round. I needed these skills to become habits, not tasks I had to consciously worry about remembering in the middle of a debate.

I needed to remember to come up with crossfire questions that expanded beyond the evidence wars. I needed to remember to restate the things the other side did wrong in summary instead of only saying everything our side did right. I needed to remember that one piece of evidence I found that worked like an automatic block to everything the opponent could possibly say.

I think what I didn't understand while I was practicing for the next tournament is that not every debater becomes perfect once they finally learn how to do casewriting and give refutations. No debater can genuinely achieve that final pedestal that stands high above the clouds, because every judge finds something different in every debater. Every judge likes different things, and some like the exact opposite. Some judges prefer when you stand to give your speech, while others prefer when you sit.

Essentially, what I'm trying to convey is that you can't satisfy every judge, so first satisfy yourself. You do this by creating goals.

This online tournament was in February 2023 — on my mother's birthday, actually. I felt a little bad about planning to spend six hours on my computer arguing with people about whether the U.S. federal government should ban TikTok instead of properly celebrating with my mother. But the debate tournament (with the NYC Urban Debate League) would end at 3 p.m., which would leave the entire afternoon and evening to spend with her.

I dedicate most of my success to my mom. Her efforts are the reason I even started competing in debate tournaments. Her constant push for me to stop sleeping or stop playing Roblox with my brother finally motivated me to stop being lazy. Don't worry — I still play Roblox with my brother. We all need some motivation in life. Don't judge me.

This time, I decided to work on my own instead of relying on my friends' work to help me understand. I wanted the joy of achieving comprehension on my own.

This time, I decided to structure the arguments better. This time, they weren't thin. They were fat. The evidence was bold, and the impact was dramatic — but not too over-the-top.

Now that I fully understood refutations and the horrific feeling of having to think on the spot with a blank mind, I overprepared. I wrote so many blocks that while I typed them, my brain was already thinking of blocks to the blocks.

I remember my dad telling me that I was going insane by reciting the speech I had for both sides ten times every night before I went to bed. I had to be perfect. My dad thought I was perfectly insane.

My mindset changed, though. I no longer thought I was the best at everything I did. I had to work hard to be good. Skills don't just naturally come to people. I wasn't egotistical anymore, and that was the best change I had seen in myself. I was humbled into actually thinking I needed to study for tests now.

The changes that I saw in myself weren't just in debate. They were in my academic life too.

I noticed my grades going higher because I finally knew how to write an essay without sounding like a broken record and saying the same thing repeatedly.

I got elected as class representative (coincidentally with my debate partner!) and took part in student government the next year as Secretary as well.

As I prepared for the next tournament, something I overlooked was crossfire — a time when I had to give immediate responses. Sometimes my responses weren't very good, or I just stayed in silence for a hot 30 seconds before being able to say something.

I struggled with this for the next five tournaments as well. Believe me, after this February tournament, I tried to get better at answering questions quickly, but I didn't know how to go about it, so there wasn't much progress.

Finally, the day came when I had to wake up at 7:30 in the morning and stare at my computer screen to argue with people about something that I honestly did not care about. But I had to sound like I did. I had to give all my speeches with evidence, make eye contact, and ask those little questions at the beginning of the round to make the judge think I was cool, even though I could tell they didn't care at all.

Tirelessly, I argued with people. The good thing about online debates is that when your opponent says something ridiculous, you're on mute, so you can laugh as loudly as you want.

My opponent tried to convince me that China and the United States were the best of allies. Oh, this person certainly did not read the news very often. He sure mumbled a lot too.

After the first two rounds, I knew that we had done excellently. During the lunch break, my friends and I did a FaceTime call to talk about our rounds, laugh at things people said, or rave about how annoying our opponents were.

Suddenly, I decided to check Tabroom out of boredom and saw that the pairings for the final round were released. I read out the names out loud, definitely mispronouncing one of the surnames.

My friend said "Oh shoot," slowly into the mic.

"We went against them before," she told me. "They're really good and we lost against them. They always get first place or close to first at these tournaments. But this is good news! Third round is based on how you did in the previous two rounds, so that means you definitely won the last two."

I felt a pit in my stomach.

How were we going to defeat this supposedly insurmountable team? I felt myself getting hot from stress. I recoiled in my seat and put myself on mute. I went to the living room to tell my dad our fate — our horrible luck.

My dad made a disapproving face at me. "You're always so negative. Believe in yourself. I was listening to you in the previous rounds. You are fine."

I huffed. I hated when my dad lectured me when I was already trying my best. But I decided to listen to him regardless. I wasn't going to let this inconvenience prevent me from doing my absolute best in this round. We were going to win!

"Yeah, we definitely lost that," my partner told me after the round ended. I nodded in agreement.

They absolutely crushed us with their annoying faces and annoying replies during crossfire. I felt sour about it but was sure that we did well enough to get at least a 5th place team award. That would still be amazing.

We joined the main meeting room for the award ceremony and waited as the league took their iconic amount of time to prepare everything. I'm pretty sure they were mentally preparing how to pronounce every single last name, because why do debaters have the most complicated last names ever?

As they proceeded to call out the names for the other forms of debate, I felt myself zoning out. Then, it was time for our division to be called out. I listened as they went from number 20 on the podium and moved upward. Our names weren't being called, and I felt myself growing more dreadful by the second.

Then it happened. The last names called — the names called to hold the prestige of first place — were the ones of me and my partner. I remember screaming. Not in a horrified way, but in a way that showed I was shocked and overjoyed.

This meant we had won the last round. It meant that we had actually succeeded. I felt like I understood what had changed and what I needed to put into effect for the future. I needed to maintain a new mindset of positivity. After a round ends, I am never going to feel disdain toward myself because I think I did horribly. I'm not going to think I did badly because I never do. Nobody does when they gave it their all through practice.

Practice brought me here.

My mom rushed into the room, cradling my head in her arms, and my dad called from the bathroom, confused.

Later, when my dad came into the room, he looked at me with a straight face, eyes slightly bulging.

"There's no way you won. You must have heard it wrong, I'm telling you."

"No, I heard it correctly, I'm telling you!"

For the first time ever, I actually felt like I genuinely achieved something. This was my first award that I had ever won in anything. Everyone had different reasons for starting debate and for doing debate. I started debate because I wanted to impress my parents with a feat I knew was achievable. But now I was doing debate because I realized I found some kind of purpose and joy in it — a purpose and joy that I couldn't find anywhere else.

I think the thrill that I found in debate was beyond just pointing out where people were wrong. The topics were always interesting to me. I didn't know anything about the NSA and Edward Snowden, but now I do, and I want to learn more about the United States' national security and how I am affected by decisions.

That was the second thrill I found in debate. I learned that current events were actually more important than I originally thought because debate showed me how government decisions impacted me directly and on large scales. I learned that even though I don't use social media, a ban on it could still affect my lifestyle.

I might sound cringey for saying that I found a love in learning, but I think debate is a good way to teach inside the classroom as well. I found myself confident and ready whenever the teacher said anything close to "respectful disagreements." Whether you like it or not, you are going to be debating in the classroom with the common exercise of standing around the room based on your opinions.

But debate also led to something outside of the academic world: friends!

3

Your Opponent is Not Your Worst Enemy

I think one of the main reasons I got really into debate was because I made some spectacular friends along my middle school journey. I entered my debate career without really anticipating that I could make friends through it. Honestly, I thought debate tournaments were going to be really serious and would just be a repeat of competing against random kids that I would never see again.

I was very wrong.

Once you're part of a debate league, you honestly build a community and a reputation for yourself. At every tournament, I realized I was seeing the same kids giggling with their teams, the same ones getting boba from a mysterious source on the Columbia campus, and the same ones I had actually competed against. I like to say that the debate world is quite small because I ended up debating the same students again and again, and that built a nice friendship for me. I also saw kids who had transferred from my school to others. It made me realize that New York City had a lot more to offer than what was within the walls of my public school.

I didn't really know how to make friends outside of school because I thought it was always going to be a given for me. I planned to be at this school from kindergarten through 8th grade, and I assumed we'd all probably go to the same high school, so I didn't think it mattered. It wasn't that deep, and I didn't feel like I needed to make friends elsewhere. What would I even talk to them about? More debate?

I remember one girl who I met at the NYC Urban Debate League Championships in 8th grade. That year, I decided to shift debate styles for a while to get the whole "middle school" experience while I still could, because I knew Spence — the high school I was going to — only had a Public Forum debate team. I couldn't compete in Parliamentary there even if I wanted to.

Luckily, I found a team of two great people who honestly made debate really memorable. The two of us actually did work, while the third scheduled dates with Minecraft. Will and Alex made debate unforgettable with our goofy Google Meets the day before every tournament in 8th grade, and by being locked in at the actual tournaments.

I felt loyalty through my partners, and that mattered to me. Loyalty, dynamic, and having a relationship beyond debate were really important, especially since I went to a relatively small middle school (64 kids per grade). If I worked with someone and didn't talk to them often, I felt like an outsider to them. I wanted to make friends and get to know people well.

As for dynamic, I believed that you and your partners shouldn't be good at all the same things or weak at all the same things. Nobody benefits from that. You need a partner who can balance you out. But this doesn't mean you should avoid potential partners just because they have the same strengths and weaknesses. In fact, I partnered with my best friends Angela and Kayla twice in 8th grade in Public Forum tournaments at Youth for Debate at Columbia University. Both times, we placed tremendously — 2nd and 3rd place — even though we had many of the same abilities (but they're always the best of the best).

Loyalty is also important. You need a partner who does the work and contributes. I've been in partnerships where one partner did everything while the other lived life in the name of "having fun." Will, Alex, Angela, and Kayla never abandoned me when I needed them to work on debate, and that helped me a lot.

But I had also been surrounded by the same people for nine years (kindergarten through 8th grade), which made everyone extremely close — maybe too close. Sometimes, it made me feel like I didn't know how to make friends elsewhere.

At debate tournaments, I tried to get to know other people with stupid conversation starters like, "What's your favorite Labubu?" or "Do you like K-pop?"

Sometimes, while waiting for the judge who was late by an hour, we played Brawl Stars with our opponents and prank-called Tabroom support a couple of times. Don't worry, Tabroom was pretty chill with us and asked if we were winning in Brawl Stars. Sometimes, I even became friends with the judges. I remember one judge in particular who dressed up in a cow costume during the award ceremony. He was a very silly yet serious college student.

I also remember another girl clearly — her insanely curly hair and pretty smile. I suddenly remembered that I had competed against her at a previous tournament. The debate world was so small.

"Hey, I remember we debated against each other before," I said with a laugh. "I'm Bani."

"Oh yeah, I remember you," she said, introducing herself.

I noticed her team had changed slightly — one new person and one familiar face from a previous tournament, a short boy I remembered.

We bonded in between rounds (and during that iconic long wait that the Urban Debate League always has at the start of tournaments). We talked about horrible past debate experiences with annoying opponents who were present at that very tournament.

Before the semifinals, the short boy came up to us and grinned.

"Imagine if we both get to compete against each other in the finals," he said. "I'd rather compete against you than compete against [redacted]."

Imagine my surprise when fate brought us both to the finals.

At first, I was slightly nervous, but as the round progressed, I remembered that I had dreamed of this happening — that we *would* meet in finals.

We all debated fiercely, both sides doing excellently. I liked the motion because I remembered that in 6th grade social studies, we had the same topic for a class project. I felt well prepared — except for the fact that we had a hard-to-defend side.

The motion was about returning historically stolen artifacts to their home countries, and we had to argue why that shouldn't happen. I felt uneasy, but a friend from a different division helped us think of arguments.

Before the girl's speech, I felt that we had a good chance of winning. After, I felt the final could go either way. She spoke with emphasis and confidence — it was no wonder she had earned 1st place speaker that day (I had gotten 4th place!).

When the judges announced the 2-1 decision in our favor, I felt overjoyed. We had won the city championships for a debate format that I didn't even specialize in. But there was still room for improvement — one judge still found the other side more persuasive. Even if we had gotten all three judges to vote for us, there still would've been feedback to help us grow.

This tournament made me feel more confident in my speaking abilities and allowed me to conclude my Parliamentary career strong.

I remembered the beginning of my debate journey. I used to be terrified of speaking even a little bit extemporaneously. I used to write half of my summary speeches beforehand and use a bunch of prep time to finish the rest. I didn't even weigh in summary speech — I didn't know what that was. But now, here I am in April of 2025, spending almost half of my speech weighing without stuttering, fumbling, or being completely intimidated by my opponent.

Being intimidated by my opponent did happen several times at the championship tournament, actually. We had gone against the same team twice in a row, and they were honestly the other best team in the division. I was scared because we had debated them twice before (my teammates even more than me). We had won once out of those two times, and both rounds had been really close.

One of the girls on that team was quite aggressive in debate — not in a violating way, but intimidating. Her heckles and Points of Information (POIs) were known to be really demanding. I had practice in crossfire from Public Forum, so why was I terrified?

To be honest, Public Forum is a much more respectful form of debate than Parliamentary. In Parliamentary, people often try to cut each other off for speaker points, and it becomes uncomfortable. The spontaneity of questions threw me off and often made me glitch in my speaking.

The tournament that followed — where I competed with my best friend Angela — was also filled with happiness and long sessions of waiting for judges, playing Brawl Stars with our opponents.

How joyous!

II

Part Two

The second part of this book goes into depth about each part of the debate structure. Please acknowledge that timings of speeches vary from league to league and the timings I mention in the chapters are the ones I've used in my debate career as well. Throughout these chapters, I will not only cover the basic burdens of each speech but some secret tips that have led me to win rounds solely based off of them. Do not rely completely on these tips to win rounds because it all depends on execution!

4

Public Forum but Better

As interesting as my debate stories are, it's time to actually get into the nitty-gritty of debate. Public Forum is more of an evidence- and impact-based debate, while other forms of debate are all about finding solutions (like parliamentary debate) or more.

This means that you don't need to focus your research so much on trying to find other propositions that could be beneficial and rather just prove your arguments for why the proposition being debated is detrimental or not in the larger scheme of things.

Additionally, it means that you need to have an impact that expands beyond the analysis of your evidence because that is a frequent expectation in debate.

Public Forum tends to be a more organized form of debate as well, with allocated times for opponents to ask questions to each other instead of interrupting in the middle of speeches as other debate formats encourage.

Another reason I love Public Forum is that it also places emphasis on speaking ability instead of spreading at lightning speed. *Spreading* is speaking extremely fast in order to fit more material within the time constraint of the speech. You probably won't encounter spreading until high-school debate.

Format of a Public Forum Debate Round

Affirmative Constructive (Speaker 1)	3 minutes
Negative Constructive (Speaker 1)	3 minutes
Crossfire (Speaker 1)	2 minutes
Affirmative Rebuttal (Speaker 2)	3 minutes
Negative Rebuttal (Speaker 2)	3 minutes
Crossfire (Speaker 2)	2 minutes
Affirmative Summary Speech (Speaker 1)	2 minutes
Negative Summary Speech (Speaker 2)	2 minutes
Grand Crossfire (All Speakers)	2 minutes
Affirmative Final Focus (Speaker 2)	2 minutes
Negative Final Focus (Speaker 2)	2 minutes

In total, a debate round is 26 minutes of mandatory speaking time. With the added two minutes of prep time for each side, it becomes between 26 and 30 minutes (depending on how much prep time each side uses). Depending on leagues, the timing of each speech can be different!

As you can see in the chart above, there are two speakers for each team in a Public Forum debate round. Each speaker responds to their Affirmative/Negative counterpart in their speech (except for the constructive speech).

The first speaker in Public Forum does more of the pre-written speaking, like the contentions and the summary speech. Even though the summary speech is half extemporaneous, it is still essentially set up by the material prepared in the constructive speech.

The second speaker in Public Forum does more of the extemporaneous speaking and crystallizing for the judge to see who really wins more. The offense and defense that the second speaker plays are critical to actually spark the debate.

The judge has an equally important role as the speakers. Their ability to examine which team genuinely does better in a debate round is something to be praised because sometimes it can be really hard to decide the winner of a round. To make that decision, you need good flowing skills.

Additionally, it is the judge's job to make sure that the speakers are debating well and not being impolite or offensive to each other. It's also their job to listen carefully to which points were responded to and which were not. People often underestimate the judge as an annoying person, but they're the reason that debate tournaments can actually happen!

Constructive Speech

The first part of Public Forum debate is the constructive speech. In the constructive speech, each side presents their contentions regarding their stance on the resolution.

There are usually around 2–3 contentions per side. I remember in my earlier debate days, I used two contentions but slowly started shifting to three when I learned how to use each and every second in a three-minute timeframe.

Each argument usually follows the format **AREI**, which stands for

Assertion, Reasoning, Evidence, Impact.

The constructive speech is given by the first speaker. It is important that you do NOT respond to your opponent's constructive speech in your constructive speech — save that for crossfire and the rebuttal speech.

Crossfire

After the constructive speeches are given by both sides, the first speakers engage in the first crossfire of the round.

Crossfire is the allocated question-and-answer period I was referring to earlier. Usually, most people are very timid during this period, and more time is spent waiting in silence for the other person to speak than actually speaking.

But when that doesn't happen, the two sides argue over one or two questions the entire time instead of respectfully sticking to asking and answering — but the judges often find thrill in it. They love the clash, so don't back down!

Rebuttal Speech

After the first crossfire, the second speakers both give their respective rebuttal speeches. The rebuttal speech is where both sides point out what is wrong with each other's arguments.

Most people don't know this, but I really like to *weigh* during the rebuttal speech. Weighing is when someone compares the impacts of the arguments of the two sides.

For weighing, debaters commonly use the mechanisms below:

a) **Scope** — How many people your impact reaches.

b) **Magnitude** — How severe your impact is.

c) **Timeframe** — Will your side's proposition work in the long term? Is it more time-efficient? (There are two ways to use the timeframe mechanism.)

d) **Probability** — Is their impact improbable? Your impact has a greater probability of happening.

e) **Utilitarianism** — Your impact affects the greatest number of people in the biggest way.

There are more weighing mechanisms than these "Big Five," but these are the ones that judges look for the most.

A common mistake when using these mechanisms is only demonstrating how your arguments impact a group of people but not comparatively weighing both sides on a mechanism. In the word "weighing," we can kind of picture a scale with two things on each side — that helps us remember to weigh both teams' arguments, not just one.

Second Crossfire

After the rebuttal speeches, there is the second crossfire between the second speakers of each side.

In this crossfire, competitors usually ask questions directed at the rebuttal speech just given, because this is when some of the real clash starts happening — both sides have now responded to each other's points.

Sometimes, opponents notice that the other team didn't refute one of their arguments, so they point it out in crossfire, emphasizing that the other team had no response. This directly shows your opponent could not think of a way to prove your argument wrong.

Summary Speech

After this crossfire, the wonderful summary speech done by the first speakers takes place.

In the summary speech, it's a little frustrating that you get only 2–3 minutes to summarize not only your arguments but your opponents' as well and explain so much that happened during the round. So, when you have so much to explain, how do you make sure your speech doesn't sound like a jumble of words being thrown around but instead sounds well-structured?

Firstly, in the summary speech, you need to summarize your arguments with one sentence for each reason and then one sentence to summarize the impacts of all of your reasons — reminding the judge of the importance of your arguments and why they still should be taken into account.

After that, you have to restate the refutations that the other side had against your reasons and rebuild your arguments in response to their attacks. *Rebuilding* is a debate term for refuting your opponent's refutation to one of your arguments.

An example I like to give is that your argument is a tower. When your opponent refutes your argument, your tower falls apart. You need to rebuild your tower by playing defense and showing that your opponent's refutation is invalid.

After you rebuild, you have to go to their arguments and summarize them lightly. Then, refute them! This shows the judge that their arguments are weak while yours are still strong because you rebuilt them.

After this, you conclude the speech with weighing.

Grand Crossfire

Following the summary speeches is the Grand Crossfire, in which all four speakers in the round converse instead of only the first speakers or only the second speakers.

During the Grand Crossfire, the judge looks for all four competitors to participate instead of certain people taking over the entire crossfire — which actually happens quite frequently. This way, the judge is assured that all speakers are confident in their ability to answer questions extemporaneously.

Final Focus

The last part of a debate round is the final focus.

The final focus is the last word from each side, and within it, each side crystallizes the arguments given in the debate. This means that each side makes it crystal clear to the judge who should win by collapsing the arguments into what impact the judge should acknowledge the most.

Debaters often phrase it like, "This debate boils down to ____," or something along those lines. The majority of the final focus is spent weighing.

Now that we've lightly examined each part of the debate round, it makes us pose the question: if everyone does these things the correct way, how does the judge make the decision?

Judges look for a lot of things in debate — it's not all about what is in your speech but also how you present it to the judge and opponents. Great speaking means emphasizing key parts of your speech (but obviously don't emphasize everything – you'll sound excessive). Emphasizing key parts — the impact or big statistics in your evidence — helps the judge keep listening and encourages them to write it down on their flow.

Flowing is a form of note-taking in debate that not only the judge does but also the competitors. This is important because flowing does not capture everything that a person says (it's called *flowing*, not *scribbling down everything!*). Flowing captures the main arguments with important subpoints that the opponent makes.

I like to include refutations next to the arguments as part of my flow because that allows me to see the "flow" in my thoughts when I give a refutation speech later.

This is also important for the judge to do because it clearly lets them see that each side replied to all the points mentioned by the other.

Additionally, when flowing, it's good to know what you're capable of. If you know you can't give a speech with just a few bullet points, then don't be afraid to write some of it out.

Back to speaking — it is important that you make good eye contact with the judge. This seems like a very basic requirement at first, but even in my debate experience, when I make strong eye contact with the judge, they still ask for more (there's always room to improve, so don't beat yourself up over feedback from judges).

Additionally, it's good to always include a little extemporaneous speaking. Yes, each team is given two minutes of prep time, but don't waste all of it writing out a speech word for word — that's inefficient.

I suggest using around 30 seconds for rebuttal (only if you need it), 30–45 seconds for the summary speech, and the rest for the final focus. In this amount of time, you can make bullet points to remind yourself of your train of thought and maintain eye contact with the judge, earn higher speaker points for extemporaneous delivery, and not waste prep time!

Benefits

This may seem very confusing at first, but there are a lot of reasons why debate can help you not only in the debate room but also in many other areas of your daily life.

As a student, when I started debate, I found myself able to manage my time much better because I knew I needed to balance the schedule of my extracurriculars with my schoolwork. This made me start creating a schedule for debate to make sure I did just enough work each day instead of spending hours on it all at once.

I know what you might be thinking: "Bani, isn't it better to get more work done faster?" No, it's not. Essentially, that deprives each part of your preparation of the proper amount of attention it needs.

Time is time. If you're spending too much time on one section, you're overthinking it, getting stressed, and limiting the amount of time you spend on other sections. You might get all the work done eventually, but you'll be forcing it into a time constraint.

If you're spending too little time on one section, then it's not going to be as strong as your other parts. You want to make sure that the evidence is just as persuasive as the impact and that you have no overlooked holes for opponents to poke through.

Another reason debate is good for students is because it builds critical presentational and collaborative skills. These skills are crucial in the future workforce — and especially if you're looking to get admitted into high school or college, schools love to see you developing skills through things you love to do (like debate!).

Additionally, these skills help within the classroom as well — with inevitable group projects, presentations, and writing well-structured essays.

The list of benefits goes on!

5

Casewriting

We briefly covered in the previous chapter the necessity of having well-structured arguments in the constructive speech.

Arguments, or *contentions* in debate-speak, follow a certain structure called the **AREI format**:

A — **Assertion**

R — **Reasoning**

E — **Evidence**

I — **Impact**

This may sound very simple to follow, but there are a lot of do's and don'ts when writing strong contentions that your opponent will have trouble refuting.

Firstly, for the assertion, it's best to keep it short and straightforward.

Example: *"We affirm the resolution which states that school uniforms should not be banned."*

This shows your side and the resolution that you are asserting. A pro tip is to make this part of your off-time roadmap — a small outline of what you're going to say before your speech starts — so you have more time dedicated to your actual contentions and not formal introductions. So really, you're following more of an **REI** format during the speech.

Next is the **reasoning**. Most debaters spend around 30 seconds summarizing their entire argument in their reasoning, but little do they know that it's unnecessary and wastes valuable time. Judges want you to get straight to the point so they can write your reasons on their flow. It's best to have a short tagline for your reason instead of writing a whole paragraph explaining it. You can elaborate when you present your evidence — that way, you are bringing something new to the table.

Example: *Our first contention is the economic benefits.*

See how simple that is? Without going in-depth in our reasoning, we can allow our evidence to contribute what we were going to include, but backed with statistics and examples cited from articles. This demonstrates a connection and sets us up for the impact.

For the **evidence** part, many people get confused about what really qualifies as a strong piece of evidence.

Many debaters, when desperate, choose evidence that just restates the reasoning or cherry-picks a weak example, which the opponent can easily point out. Good evidence includes **statistics**, because unlike individual examples, they demonstrate a general **trend** and easily set us up for the impact. Additionally, good evidence often includes information **not already widely known**.

For example, if the topic is federally banning TikTok and one of the arguments is "China collects the data of many U.S. citizens," it would be better to demonstrate *how* they do that and *how* it affects people individually or on a larger scale.

However, this doesn't mean examples are bad. They can be great —

especially when they illustrate an effect on a group of people (though avoid using just one person's experience, since that can be labeled as cherry-picking).

It's quite hard to retain evidence that goes in-depth like this, and with that comes **good researching**. A good researcher does **not** type the entire resolution into the search bar and click the first few articles. A good researcher types in the **keywords** from their reasons, not the full resolution, and looks at a variety of results.

Additionally, they keep track of all the articles they've gone through on a Google Doc to ensure they can cite sources properly in their speech. Remember to keep an open mind in your research. Even if you come across a substantial piece of evidence that doesn't support your argument, save it — you might need it for a block. Don't only focus on the particular reason you're researching at that exact moment.

For some extra tips on evidence, it's good to **cut down** large chunks of text. Articles often use filler words and transitions that will waste time in your speech. You want to *cut to the chase.* Don't be afraid to remove sentences, because many will be irrelevant to your specific point.

In Chapter 1, I talked about how hard it was for me to decide what to delete. Remember, you're not really deleting anything — you're embedding and connecting it to the main arguments. This is thinking smarter, not harder.

Here's an example of a well-structured piece of evidence that thoroughly supports the reason:

> **R:** We affirm because AI can personalize learning and convert materials to be accessible to all children, including those with disabilities.
>
> **E:** According to "Using Artificial Intelligence in Education: Pros and Cons" by The Knowledge Review, "AI can optimally introduce courses and challenge students based on

their strengths and weaknesses. Kidaptive and Century Tech are platforms developed exclusively to offer individualized learning plans to students. They can also perform predictive analysis on the academic performance of pupils based on the underlying patterns. AI is playing a crucial role in improving the lives of the disabled. Speech recognition software such as Nuance can help transcribe words for students with writing difficulties or limited mobility. These solutions can help teachers offer better study materials for students that attend to their unique demands like never before." Also, according to The Journal, "With AI, students now have a personalized approach to learning programs based on their own unique experiences and preferences. AI can adapt to each student's level of knowledge, speed of learning and desired goals so they're getting the most out of their education. AI-powered solutions can analyze students' previous learning histories, identify weaknesses and offer courses best suited for improvement."

We can see that the piece of evidence here doesn't just repeat the point I'm trying to make — it *proves it* with valid examples of AI mechanisms. It also explains what these AI mechanisms do in depth, *how* they do it, and demonstrates the link to my case.

Finally, for the **impact**, it's important to analyze your evidence and demonstrate why the judge should take this argument seriously. Bring your impact to the next level. Don't focus solely on a small scope. This is how you foreshadow weighing mechanisms that you will use later in the debate. It also makes your weighing job easier and shows the judge that you put real thought into your casewriting.

Here's an example:

TOPIC: *Social media should be federally banned for those under 13*

REASON: *Social media harms the cognitive development of children at an early age*

IMPACT: Judge, these preteens are the next generation of workers. Not only does this issue have devastating individual effects, widespread poor mental health also has significant societal costs, meaning that our national economy can face risks. This includes increased healthcare expenses, reduced productivity, strain on social services, and a general decrease in overall societal well-being.

See how this impact expands beyond the individual effect of cognitive development and connects to a more serious issue — the future economy being at risk? This is one of many ways to write an impact in a way that the judge can weigh over your opponent's arguments.

This impact can also set you up for weighing later in the round, using mechanisms like **long-term**, **scope**, and **magnitude**, because the effects are widespread (the entire economy) and long-lasting.

This may seem like a lot to take in at first, but for me, it ended up becoming natural through practice and competing in many tournaments. That experience helped me develop a reliable framework for writing each part of a contention. The same will likely happen for you.

Don't feel scared to put yourself out there with weak arguments. Remember my first debate tournament? I only had one argument — and I didn't do so bad!

6

Rebuttal Speech

The rebuttal speech, delivered by the second speaker, essentially has to prove the opponent wrong.

We touched on this speech briefly in Chapter 4, but there is much more to know than just "proving your opponent wrong" and weighing the impacts of your speech and your opponents' speech.

Most debaters follow a certain format when trying to refute each claim their opponent makes. Often, it will sound something like this:

> *"My opponent's first contention was _____, but Judge, they're not considering that _____."*

This is a very basic format, and it's always best to deliver your refutations in the **same order your opponent presented their arguments**. This makes it easy for the judge to tick off each argument you refuted on their flow, without hunting for it or tuning out of your speech.

In addition to the format above, it's always best to **include evidence** to support your refutation. Before the debate, you should have done extensive research and saved it on your document (if you're researching correctly!), and you can use that evidence in your rebuttal.

If you don't have something new, then refer back to evidence in your constructive speech. This can be extremely effective! Judges love when you reference your constructive evidence because it reinforces that your earlier arguments were meaningful and deserve to be weighed in their decision.

Lastly, **conclude each individual refutation with impact**. Show how their argument does *not* have as significant an impact as yours. This directly compares both sides' cases and sets up future weighing.

You might notice that rebuttal structure sounds familiar — it's like **AREI**, but for proving someone wrong, and much shorter!

Don't feel that your refutations must only apply to each argument as a whole — it's also great to **poke holes in sub-points**. Depending on the judge's values, small holes can sometimes carry a lot of weight. So, what exactly can you poke holes in?

It's actually ideal to have a *mix* of full-argument refutations and sub-point refutations, because it builds **more clash** — which is something judges love. Clash is when you and your opponent directly argue about a specific element of a case. It is very important to have clash, especially because it sets up your **Final Focus** later. In Final Focus, you must prove why you win on key points of clash.

Common Sub-Point Refutation Targets

1) Irrelevant quotes or arguments

Often, debaters use arguments that don't actually relate to the resolution. This may not always be obvious, which is why it's important to listen carefully to the wording of their claim.

For example, if the resolution is about AI in **K–12 education in the United States,** and their evidence concerns college students or AI in another country, that evidence is irrelevant. Pointing this out shows that the foundation of their argument is weak.

However — and this is VERY important — do **not** rely on the cheap tactic of attacking the *source* just because it isn't a university or well-known organization. That type of refutation shows you cannot attack the *logic* of the argument. Only point out source credibility issues when you truly have no other option.

If someone uses this attack on *your* source, respond by either:

· providing an additional source that reinforces your claim, **or**
· emphasizing that your point is grounded in sound logic, not just citation.

2) Asking for a solution

If your opponent asks, "Well, what's YOUR solution?" simply respond that it is not your burden. There is **no rule** in Public Forum debate that requires either side to provide a solution. That's a feature of *parliamentary debate*, not Public Forum.

3) Personal stories as evidence

If your opponent uses a personal anecdote, it can be tricky to refute because you don't want to sound insensitive. However, anecdotes are **not valid evidence** in Public Forum.

The best, most respectful response is:

"I'm sorry that happened to you, but with all due respect, personal anecdotes can't be used as evidence in Public Forum debate."

These are just **three common targets**, but there are many other ways to poke holes in arguments.

Blocks

Rebuttals can be hard to think of in the moment, so I strongly recommend writing **blocks** — pre-written refutations. Blocks save a lot of prep time and reduce stress. Set aside time to write blocks on a consistent basis and make them strong.

Don't just write blocks for arguments you *expect* opponents to run — write blocks against **your own arguments**, too. If your argument was good enough for you to think of, someone else may be running it as well. Writing refutations to your own points will help you strengthen them ahead of time.

Teamwork in Rebuttal

When thinking of refutations in-round, don't be afraid to quietly ask your partner for help. Whisper a question, pass a sticky note, or point to a gap on the flow. Partnership means thinking **together**, not suffering in silence. Multiple perspectives often create better, cleaner refutations — and prevent those awkward silent pauses mid-speech. This is also why block-writing is great to do with your partner!

These habits also help increase your **speaker points**.

Avoid This Major Mistake

Do **not** reply to every argument using the **same exact sentence or phrase**, even if it technically applies to all of them. If your opponent successfully rebuilds against that one sentence, they have knocked out your entire rebuttal in one hit.

It also shows:

· lack of creativity

- lack of evidence
- repetitive delivery

The judge gets bored, and your opponent gets stronger. Avoid that. Remember, you can — and should — refer back to your case during rebuttal. It shows you are not only playing defense, but also reinforcing offense.

Sample Refutation

Here is an example (not a full rebuttal speech):

> *"Judge, our opponent is talking about short-term economic downturns, but our side is focused on the future and the long term. In our contentions, we explained that our future economy is at risk when students today dedicate most of their time to social media, which harms their mental health and slows cognitive development. We cited the NIH study, which states:*
>
> 'Brain development is a critical factor to consider. Adolescents are undergoing a highly sensitive period of brain development when risk-taking behaviors reach their peak, when well-being experiences the greatest fluctuations, and when mental health challenges such as depression typically emerge. In early adolescence, when identities and sense of self-worth are forming, brain development is especially susceptible to social pressures, peer opinions, and peer comparison. Social media use may be associated with distinct changes in the developing brain in the amygdala (important for emotional learning and behavior) and the prefrontal cortex (important for impulse control, emotional regulation, and moderating social behavior).'"

7

Summary Speech

I feel like the summary speech is my favorite part of debate because you're essentially showing the Judge everything important that happened in the round while also giving yourself a little clarity as well.

In a debate round, a lot can be going on, and sometimes in crossfire, debaters get sidetracked and focus on elements that aren't really important in the grand scheme of things, like evidence sources. The summary speech is basically a breather from everything that happened. It shows the Judge what they *actually* should be focusing on when making their decision.

This is also a speech where you're not playing tricks — you're not twisting words or misrepresenting evidence. You are plainly summarizing what occurred on both sides.

I stated in chapter 4 that you need to essentially have a checklist of everything you must accomplish in the summary speech. Let's go a little more in depth on the elements we brushed over.

Before we begin, I want to remind you that the summary speech is **NOT** a repeat of the constructive speech. You should not be restating all your arguments again. A summary is a *brief* recount of your contentions.

Firstly, we discussed that you need to summarize your own arguments. Do not restate entire pieces of evidence or impact. You should state each reason and then, afterward, include **one sentence to sum up the impact of all of them**. If you found a piece of evidence that was really helpful in your rebuttal or during crossfire, you may bring it up — but do not restate the entire citation. And remember to add a line of impact and explain **why it weighs for your side**.

It might seem counterintuitive, but after this part, you need to state the refutations that your opponent made to your contentions. If they failed to refute one or more of your arguments, point that out! But don't ignore or gloss over the refutations they *did* make, because those matter. The Judge needs a clear understanding of how they attempted to attack your points so that you can **rebuild** your arguments in response.

Remember the castle metaphor I gave earlier? This is that part.

You need to rebuild your arguments properly. Don't just rebuild against the refutations from the rebuttal speech. If they weighed against a particular argument, rebuild that. If they poked a hole during crossfire, rebuild that. If they refuted your previous refutations, rebuild that too!

Do **not** spend time rebuilding against a refutation that already passed and was already discussed. If you do, you're wasting time and giving the impression that you're avoiding the more recent clash — which signals to the Judge that your opponent has the upper hand on that point.

Now that your arguments have been protected, it's time to **attack the other team's case**. State each of their contentions and explain how you refuted them. If they already rebuilt, then refute *their latest version*, not their old one. If you don't refute the newest update of their contention, then you're not truly refuting it — you're acting like the previous round of clash didn't happen.

It's also okay to refute subpoints that were major clash points in the round. You must keep up with the clash because clash is one of the most important elements of debate. Clash is *practically the debate*. You may use evidence again if needed, but remember not to re-quote lengthy lines, because the next part is more important: **weighing**.

After you summarize your arguments, rebuild them, and refute your opponents' arguments, it's time to **weigh everything**. It is critical that you get to at least **one** weighing point before time is up, because weighing is one of your burdens in the summary speech. It is mandatory.

Do's and Don'ts of Summary Speech

DO: Bring in at least *some* line of evidence. This is called **extending** your argument. It is better to use evidence at this point than to simply say, *"We rebuilt, so our argument still stands."*

DON'T: Introduce brand-new clash points. Refutation and crossfire are the proper times to introduce clash. Summary is too late, and bringing up new material wastes valuable time. Remember — it's a **SUMMARY**, not "a whole new speech."

DO: Roadmap and signpost instead of repeating every tagline. For your offtime roadmap, say that you will cover:

1. Your arguments
2. Rebuild them
3. Refute your opponents' arguments
4. Weigh

> Do **not** give specifics in your offtime roadmap, because that's cheating and not allowed. Signposting — statements like "My first contention was..." or "Their second contention was..." — may seem small, but they are hugely important. The Judge must be able to follow you with absolute clarity.

DON'T: Lose track of time. If there is **one** speech you must time, it is summary. You have many burdens, so time management is crucial. A suggested pacing could be:

- 10 seconds to summarize your arguments
- 10 seconds to restate the impact
- 45 seconds to address their refutations and rebuild
- 30 seconds to summarize and refute their contentions
- Remaining time for weighing

But never rush your words. If you do not reach weighing, it's okay — just make sure it is **emphasized in Final Focus**.

You definitely have summary speech in the bag. Trust yourself. You should use prep time unless you are 100% prepared and confident. Judges tend to feel skeptical if you take *no* prep, because it signals that you are either not trying your best or don't know how to manage prep time.

Sample Summary Speech

Judge, you would see that our reasoning is more favorable since the Affirmative stated that we should increase the production of nuclear energy because it will generate more jobs in the industry. But we refuted that by saying that this is putting more people in places where they are at risk to the harms of the radiation. We should not be putting more and more people in harmful conditions. Our opponent says that this is all worth it but we believe that thousands of priceless human lives should not be taken for an energy source that is dangerous.

The Affirmative also stated that using nuclear energy would end climate change, but we refuted that by saying nuclear energy pollutes because of the waste it produces and uranium mining. Judge, in our response to our argument about how poorly nuclear power is managed, our opponent said that the waste produced is relatively small. But, Judge, we should acknowledge that by increasing the amount of nuclear power plants, we are increasing the amount of waste produced, therefore increasing the amount of radiation and increasing the amount of lives lost.

Additionally, in response to our second argument about uranium mining and the threats it poses, our opponent said that it was worth it. But, Judge, our side does not believe in taking away priceless human lives for an energy source that would be ineffective and doesn't improve quality of life. Priceless human lives are not worth it. Therefore, our arguments still stand.

In addition, Judge, we win on scope and magnitude because we care about the safety of all American citizens, including those who would be near the nuclear power plants such as Black people and Navajo people. The impact of a nuclear mishap is severe and could tear the fabrics of our economy. We should not be careless and put more and more nuclear power plants on American soil because that means more people being exposed, more people dying, and more people at risk of a nuclear accident. Thank you, Judge, and we urge you to vote for the Negative, the side that cares about the health of all of our citizens."

This summary speech is the exact one I recited at a tournament, so now you can see an example of an actual refutation. Even though it didn't follow the ideal structure I recommend, I included it because of its content. The signposting and the order in which I responded allowed the judges to navigate the round from *my* perspective — which is your ultimate goal in summary speech.

8

Final Focus

F inal focuses are arguably one of the most difficult speeches to give in the debate round. They are the last impression on the Judge and your final chance to save the round for your team. This speech alone can change the entire course of the debate, which is why you want your final focus to be as impressive as possible.

We lightly touched on the topic of crystallizing before, but how do you actually do it? Essentially, you have to condense everything said in the round into **one factor of impact**. Don't confuse this with weighing — weighing is a separate part of the final focus. Crystallizing means taking the entire round and boiling it down to the single most important point. This can be a subset of your arguments or an entire reason on its own, but never make it something trivial like evidence that both sides clashed on repeatedly. It's trivial for a reason.

Then, go over all your arguments and explain the refutations the opponent made and **why you still won on each argument**. This is important because it demonstrates both defense and offense.

Additionally, point out everything your opponent **did not do**. For example:

- Did they refute all your points?
- Did they give a valid response to everything in crossfire?
- Did they provide substantial statistics instead of cherry-picking evidence?
- Did they weigh *comparatively?*

Lastly, weigh. Don't just repeat the same weighing mechanisms you used in summary speech — bring in **new weighing mechanisms**. This prevents repetition and shows that you are not stalling for time. You may also refute the weighing your opponent used in their summary.

This might *sound* like a small list of tasks, but remember you only have **two minutes**, so you must emphasize everything (without being overdramatic) to ensure that the Judge writes it down on their flow.

For close rounds, it can be very difficult to prove that you are better than the other team — especially if you have the disadvantage of being the first to give the final focus. The best advice here is to **stay organized**. Do not lose your cool by trying to re-refute every argument the other side made. Like I said earlier, condense the round into one main point and show clearly who won that point.

Remember: in final focus, you are **not allowed** to bring up new refutations or new evidence. It is unfair to both teams to introduce something new when no one has any speech left to respond. That is exactly why the rule exists — and honestly, it's just rude to break it.

However, I do have a small trick. If the opponent forgets to refute something, I don't bring it up until final focus, so they no longer have a chance to respond to it. But this only works if I have made it **very obvious to the Judge throughout the round** that my team never dropped that argument. To ensure this, in every speech you must restate your main reasons — like a small recap — to show the Judge that you consistently take all of them seriously and want them considered in the final decision.

Another tip for final focus is to **use ALL of your remaining prep time**.

Yes, you might feel ready, but unused prep time does not carry over to future rounds. It resets every round, so you might as well use it. Use it to breathe, organize bullets, talk to your partner, or think of one more angle to emphasize. Judges love when debaters use their prep time because it shows genuine effort and strategy.

Essentially, by the end of the final focus, you should see how every previous speech in the round sets you up for this moment. That is the goal. Every part of debate is interconnected, and once you truly understand **which parts of earlier speeches are supposed to set up later speeches**, that is when you will become truly successful.

III

Part Three

In this part, I will cover the inevitable obstacles in everyone's debate journey — speaking struggles and just mistakes made in the round or while casewriting. I also discuss how I grew from these mistakes in debate and just in life because debate has benefits that expand beyond from the debate room. Lastly, I go over how you can easily navigate debating opportunities close to you!

9

Say It Again, I Didn't Flow It

Nerves are normal in debate. In fact, even though I debate so much, I sometimes still shake a little while giving a speech. There are definitely a lot of speaking tips out there like "imagine the audience in their underpants" or "only imagine the person you're comfortable with," but I know these tricks don't really work for everyone or might make you laugh instead of speak formally.

Don't worry — I have some tips for you that'll calm nerves.

Firstly, splash cold water on your face or at least dab your eyes with a cold towel or tissue before the round. This calms your nerves and makes you feel less on-the-spot.

Second, use ten seconds of prep time (or whatever justified amount you want) to just **breathe**. This can be whenever you feel the most nerves or before every speech. Do whatever helps your speaking — not only your speech writing.

Third, come up with a reward system for yourself. For example, what I used to do with my partner is that after every round we would eat some Takis. As silly as this sounds, this distracts you from feeling nervous and makes you lock in on performing great in the round so you can reward yourself after. Obviously, don't make the reward system so generous for yourself that it takes your mind off the debate entirely. Be humble with yourself!

Fourth is to **do the work for you.** Often, nerves kick in when you feel that you haven't done sufficient work. To help with this, use the schedule tip I mentioned earlier! Creating a schedule for yourself helps you feel prepared enough to debate well without nerves. This helps fight procrastination as well because you're only doing a little bit of work each day instead of piling it all up and postponing it.

Additionally, you can also write out ideas in your head. If you don't want the stress of writing an entire summary speech during the round, create a fill-in-the-blank for yourself. This is like writing an outline but more specific than usual. Create an outline with all the burdens you have and then fill out the blanks during the round! This makes you feel way more prepared than you actually are because you're tricking yourself into believing you have less to stress about during the round or prep time.

Fifth is to ask your partner, coach, teammate, parent, etc., for help. Don't be afraid to do this ever — even if your helper doesn't know much about debate. Your helpers probably know a lot about you if you trust them enough to give you help. They can help you with comfort that the tips above couldn't give you.

Aside from these tips, I've dealt with fear and pressure a lot in my debate career. I've felt pressure every single time my debate coach decided to spectate one of my rounds. I felt the need to perform **stupendously** in front of him to show that I'm capable of so much. My debate coaches in middle school weren't even the scary type — in fact, they always gave me critical feedback and compliments at the end of each round they spectated. But how did I deal with this?

I forced myself to endure it. It might sound like I was a little hard on myself, but I knew that exposure was the only way that I was going to overcome this (of course, different methods work for different people, so don't follow this method if you don't want to). But I couldn't ask my coach to spectate every single one of my rounds so I could receive his feedback constantly. That would be a disrespect to my teammates. So, my father, being the supportive figure he is, spectated every single debate that he was eligible to.

I was often scared of my father watching me do things because I was scared of his judgment. But, when it came to debate, my dad just listened to what was being said in the round. He didn't sit in my view or my opponent's view, and he didn't criticize me harshly after every round like I initially thought he would. In fact, after every round he would simply just say, "You did good," and give just a sentence of advice. I've seen people do similar things and bring their closest friends to watch their debate rounds to give them that boost of confidence (but make sure you don't talk to them and laugh during debate rounds!).

After you cool your nerves, you also want to speak not only clearly but **persuasively**. You want to ensure that the Judge catches your drift and that you don't sound like a crazy person just yapping while it goes in one ear and out the other.

I've said it multiple times and I will say it again — you need to **EMPHASIZE.** I have judged numerous debate rounds and it's extremely boring when a debater talks with no feeling in their voice. I don't feel connected with the debater and I find myself trying way too hard to listen to their speech.

In debate, you are given speaker points that are on a weird scale of 25–30. A 25 is the lowest and I guarantee that you will probably never get this in your debate career unless you don't speak, spew out curse words, laugh at your opponent or with a spectator, or are a total jerk and have no etiquette. A 30 is a perfect score, but judges rarely give out this score, so don't feel too upset if you don't get one.

A **26** is a little better, but you're probably mumbling throughout your speech with a few clear parts but overall being polite to your opponent and the judges. A **27** would be presenting your arguments clearly but with no emotion and probably poor defense. A **28** would be average speaking with clarity, a little eye contact, and okay defense and offense. A **29** would include having an excellent speech structure and having an amazing ability to speak extemporaneously in crossfire.

I'll skip the obvious — don't mumble, shuffle around your papers when speaking (using a device is preferred), laugh or giggle, etc.

If I'm being completely honest, giving a debate speech is exactly like giving a presentation in front of your class, except with just a few things to emphasize more than you would to your teachers and classmates. I'm a person who has always been comfortable around most of my classmates because we've spent so many years together, but I understand that's not the case for everyone.

Even though I'm comfortable around most of my classmates, when I'm giving a presentation, I'm only really looking at my friends because their opinions are way more valuable to me than the opinions of some randoms. If that works for you, give it a try in your future tournaments, but I know it's not that easy for some people to just forget that strangers are in the room with them. I was once scared of the same judgment, so don't worry.

Here are some tips for the actual speaking in debate:

1) Stand when you're speaking. This gives you confidence, makes it easier to maintain eye contact with the Judge and opponents, and most judges actually prefer this. Why? Because most judges are lay judges, and unfortunately, in the crash course they're given at the start of the tournament, "standing" is part of the speaking criteria. But always ask the Judge before the round starts if they prefer sitting or standing during speeches. They'll give their preference and you can abide by that. If you prefer to sit down during speeches because it lets you read your notes clearly (which happens to me sometimes) and the Judge is okay with it — do that!

2) Maintain eye contact. Judges love to feel a personal connection with the debater to truly grasp the idea that they are trying to convey. Don't feel so distracted by trying to maintain eye contact that you start speaking awkwardly. Don't stare into the Judge's or opponent's souls either because it genuinely creeps them out (speaking from experience — it scares the living daylights out of me).

3) Emphasize your words. Like I said before, judges will find it more persuasive if you give the same exact speech but emphasize the important parts. Some people find this hard to do during the actual round, so I recommend bolding words in your speech beforehand that you plan to emphasize.

4) Practice makes perfect. This sounds really obvious, but most people don't do it the way they should. Practice is reciting the same speech in your room 20 times or to your partner on a call, timing yourself every time. Timing yourself is really important in the speech-writing process because you cannot have your speech go overtime. Your Judge will find it very annoying that you're not following the given rules.

You also have to make sure that you're not severely undertime. Don't rush your speech because it will ruin your clarity and make it harder for the Judge to catch everything on their flow. I remember my dad teasing me about going mentally insane before my first and second debate tournament because I practiced really hard reciting the speech.

The only person I would recite my speech to in order to get the best advice is my partner because they've been going through the speech-writing process and researching with me. Therefore, they know what elements of my speech are critical and what parts aren't. This way they can help me cut it down if I go overtime.

If you end up having extra time in your speech, I always recommend expanding on the impact of each argument a little more. Alternatively, you can restate your three reasons at the end with a conclusive statement.

Never forget to thank the Judge at the end of the speech with a cute tagline like, "and I urge you to vote for the side that cares for the economy." Sometimes, these taglines are what the Judge really remembers if they were zoning out.

You might find it a little harsh of me to always prepare for "just in case the Judge zones out!" but my debate career has been filled with judges that fell asleep during rounds at championship tournaments and judges who automatically gave you a 26 if you didn't stand while you were speaking. I had judges that were watching TikToks during the round and doing their makeup.

You have to capture the Judge's interest so they don't do these things, and you have to prepare for these situations. Make a lot of eye contact so they feel pressured to listen to you (intimidation works), and speak loudly and with emphasis.

If you want help for extemporaneous speaking, I have many lovely tips for you! Don't gatekeep these tips either because they're more fun when you do them with your entire debate team (it brings out that lovely competitive thrill).

A prep exercise that my debate team did often was to pick out two topics from a topic generator or a hat and basically come up with an invention to pitch to the investor. You have to persuade the investor within the span of a minute to invest a certain sum of money into your invention, and whichever competitor persuaded the investor the most (they received the most money from the investor) wins the game! It's like Shark Tank but very fun. This exercise trains your creativity, extemporaneous speaking, and weighing skills because you're showing your Judge how incredibly important your invention is to the betterment of humanity. This is the type of persuasion that debaters do, and it is often what the Judge bases their decision on, so it's best to train your skills by doing this.

Another prep exercise is to have one person, the moderator, stage a scenario for each person playing the game. Essentially, they set up the scenario in which you are given the topic, what your imaginary opponent has said as a refutation to one of your imaginary arguments, and you are supposed to rebuild your case based on the information given. This exercise trains extemporaneous speaking and thinking on the spot.

This third prep exercise can help you identify extremities in debate and also help you in impact writing when you're casewriting. As someone who used to hate writing impacts because I was so horrendous at it, this was very helpful. Everyone participating sits in a circle and the starting person starts with a claim such as, "Congestion pricing should be instilled in the streets of New York City," and each following person says a line of impact that supports the statement. Everyone does this continuously until someone says an extreme impact. Once they say the extreme impact, they lose and are out of the game. The game continues until there is only one person left who is declared the winner.

There are definitely more prep exercises out there that you can try out, but I always suggest doing exercises that encourage you to collaborate with your teammates, partners, or coaches instead of doing them alone. These can always be helpful in Grand Crossfire when all the speakers have to speak, because Judges really do care a lot when not all speakers in the round get a word in Grand Crossfire. It will cut down on your speaker points because it gives off the aura that you don't really know what to contribute, don't know how to respond to the opponent, and lack collaboration skills as a partnership.

10

Mistakes

M aking mistakes is one of my biggest fears, if I'm being truly honest. I'm scared of the inevitable judgment that follows. I've made many mistakes in debate. I've already told you about the time when I didn't even know that I wasn't supposed to spread out my arguments between the constructive speech and the rebuttal speech at my first tournament. But that didn't end up too horribly. We still won the round with some quick thinking. This easily demonstrates that making mistakes is okay in debate because you'll eventually get compensation — whether it be during the same round, a different one, or a different tournament entirely.

In debate, I never really made any huge mistakes apart from that, but rather a lot of small ones that I learned a lot from. Constructive criticism is one of your biggest helpers in your debate career, so you should always be open-minded to the feedback given by the judge.

I think one of the biggest mistakes of my debate career is just getting worked up in general. When I can't think of something to say in crossfire, I used to either sit in silence, say that it's actually my turn to ask the question (only when applicable, though), or awkwardly ask my partner for help. I realized that crossfire was beginning to become my least favorite part of the debate round because of its unpredictability.

But that was just the thing. I needed to make crossfire predictable and learn how to take control. I realized that my inability to reply in crossfire was due to my lack of immersing myself not only in my arguments, but also in potential arguments that could appear by researching deeper into the topic.

So how did I actually learn from this effectively? My fear of judgment pressured me to start writing blocks. I was the first speaker, so why did I need to write blocks? Why did I need to be concerned with refutations at all? Because refutations are still a critical part of summary speech and crossfire.

Crossfire is essentially a period where you not only ask and answer questions, but also foreshadow refutations and try to poke holes in your opponents' arguments. I needed to effectively target my opponents' case if I were to participate in the crossfire right after constructive speech and right before the rebuttal speech. Additionally, two perspectives are always better than one when writing and giving rebuttals. This way, our rebuttals could also be supported with evidence that we couldn't rush to find during the round or that was already in our arguments. The evidence would be new and show our judge that we had a plentiful amount of justification.

Anyways, I initiated the block-writing process. I not only wrote blocks to random potential arguments I found in articles with both sides of a case, but also to my own arguments. Like I said before, this helps structure our own arguments better, as well as helping you think of refutations in crossfire, because they will often regard the same point that you wrote blocks to (the common arguments). Eventually, you'll realize that most refutations in crossfire kind of follow a similar pattern of weighing because you're essentially arguing that the impact they described is different and would actually happen in a way that supports your side.

Another way to help this kind of freezing up is doing the prep exercises mentioned in the previous chapter.

A second common mistake that I make during debate is focusing too much on my notes and not really adapting my arguments to the judge's paradigm. I'm naturally a stubborn person and like to do things my way, or the way I prepared them to be, so when judges told me I needed a little help on this factor, I didn't want to admit that this was the very thing I was doing wrong.

A paradigm is a little blurb that you see on Tabroom next to the judge's name where the judge talks about their overall preferences for debate — including what they like to see, what they don't like debaters doing, whether or not you should stand up or sit down, and what kind of speaker points they usually give out. If your judge doesn't have a paradigm, that means they are probably, but not definitely, a lay judge — a judge who is generally new to debate and doesn't have preferences because of their lack of experience. It's best to ask them before the round starts what they like to see in debate.

Generally, what I didn't do in these situations was acknowledge the preferences but then fail to make changes on the spot to my impacts or to my weighing style in the way that they preferred it. This essentially led us to still win, but receive mediocre speaker points or harsh feedback, so we still lost in a way. So how did I really fix these mistakes without rushing before the round to delete or add things to my case?

Essentially, I needed to familiarize myself with my own case more. I did this by practicing my speech a lot — not only by myself in my room but also in practice debates with my teammates. We would always do a practice debate against each other before every tournament, with our coaches judging the round. This allows us both to get warmed up for the actual tournament and know what elements of our case were really important to stress during the actual debate round. This also helped with casewriting, as we could delete stuff that we realized hurt us more than helped us and add things that we thought our opponent did well.

In rebuttal, this basically helped us refer back to our case to create refutations. This allows us to carry all our arguments throughout the entire debate.

Debate is all about adapting. If you notice your opponent doing something great, you should kind of begin to do that too (if the judge even likes said thing). This also helps you refute your opponents' weighing. Essentially, sometimes you have to adapt your—

I haven't really made other mistakes that are greatly different from the ones described above, but there are a lot of mistakes that I found in my opponents' cases that made them incredibly easy to refute.

The biggest example of this is the usage of artificial intelligence to write the entire case. As a middle school student, I knew very well what sounded like AI and what didn't. But in debate, you can almost immediately tell that your opponent is using it if they have a combination of positive vocabulary and little to no evidence or citations supporting their case. When you type into whatever artificial intelligence chatbot you're using, the chatbot will likely just give you the argumentation, but it doesn't know how to structure it in the AREI format. Yes, you might tell it to do it that way, but it will give it to you in a long block of a speech with just a few one-liners as evidence.

Honestly, you're going to tire yourself out more by using AI and trying to make it perfect than by just writing it yourself. Additionally, what's the fun in using AI when you can't familiarize yourself with your case that well and end up losing? If I can identify it's artificial intelligence, then your judge and opponents probably can too. If you do face an opponent who uses AI, don't just straight-up point out that they did, because in the end you can't just throw accusations — it makes you look like a jerk. Essentially, you just have to show the judge that they have little to no evidence supporting their case. Additionally, since they didn't take the time to structure their arguments well on their own, the arguments will be really flawed, so just point out the flaws. The only rule is to avoid accusing them of using AI.

Another example of a mistake is not weighing comparatively. Essentially, this means that you are only weighing the impacts of your arguments and not showing how you **outweigh** your opponent on those same terms. I can say I weigh on scope and affect a large amount of people, but I need to demonstrate that my opponent affects a smaller amount of people than I do. I can say I weigh on magnitude and have a strong effect on people, but I need to demonstrate that my opponent doesn't affect people as strongly. If you're not comparing yourself to your opponent, then you aren't going to be able to make it clear to the judge who should win the round. You want to make the judge's life easier (then they'll like you better!).

A third mistake I find people often making is treating the final focus like a second summary speech or a second rebuttal. The final focus is its own speech and shouldn't be repetitive of what you said in the previous round. Like I mentioned earlier, you shouldn't be bringing in new refutations in final focus or any new material in general. Rather, you should be condensing your entire round into one point that you think should make you win the entire debate. Go back to the chapter for final focus for more tips!

A fourth mistake that I see is little to no clash. The whole point of debate is to directly compare yourself to the opponent and talk about how their points are invalid. What a lot of people do is go into crossfire unprepared to actually have clash, and it ends up being a silent waste of everybody's time. Don't make crossfire boring by sitting in silence the entire time or asking questions like, "Um... what was your third contention again?" I cannot emphasize enough how easy you're making it for the other side to win.

Yes, you might be refuting your opponents' case during the rebuttal speech, but are you actually doing any comparison in any other part of the round? Rounds like this are very boring, and you will probably get poor speaker points for not playing offense properly. So how do you actually fix this? Basically, you need to actively listen to your opponent's speech. You should've done enough research for the debate that when your opponent says something in their speech, you're starring it, underlining it — whatever you do to show that you're going to ask a question later.

A fifth mistake is just using vocabulary that attacks the debater and not the case. I know a lot of people use terminology like, "My opponent **FAILED** to do this," or "My opponent **FAILED** to do that." This is just attacking the debater and sounds really annoying if you're the opponent. I also believe these aren't the right manners in debate because, in the end, we're all just a bunch of students arguing about some random policy. It also makes you seem like an attacker to the judge, and you don't want to look like that.

There are several other mistakes that are minor but still critical. Firstly, never use hypotheticals as an example. It might be easier than finding actual real-life examples or evidence from an article, but hypotheticals are hypotheticals. They're not real and therefore not substantial evidence. Your opponent can easily call you out for not having evidence to prove your point.

Secondly, it's important not to waste your BYEs. When you look on Tabroom and see that you don't have a pairing for a round and instead a BYE, that means there is an odd number of teams at a tournament and you were chosen to sit out this round. A BYE is not guaranteed for every team. Depending on the league, this means you get a 30 for speaker points that round and a win. You're allowed to do a wide array of things during a BYE, like spectate a round or just work on your case based on the feedback that you received in a previous round.

A lot of people like to fool around during their BYEs, and this can happen even when you're not trying to. I know a lot of people just spectate other rounds but don't actually listen attentively, which defeats the purpose of spectating anyway.

Don't have your phone out while spectating, or any device. Flow on paper only, because some judges get really uncomfortable with potentially recording rounds or other forms of cheating. Flow on paper so you can keep track of your thinking better and directly mark things that you want to point out to the teammate you are spectating.

You should **ONLY** spectate teammates unless it is a final round and everyone is invited to spectate. This is just a rule in most leagues, and it's disrespectful to intrude. Always ask before you spectate as well, because even though your team might be comfortable with you spectating, the team they're debating against might not be.

Anyways, always try to flow the round because you never know if you'll have the same opponent later or go against a team from the same school (some schools do the **VERY** bad idea of all using the same arguments word for word). It has happened to me numerous times that I spectated a round and one of the debate teams was coincidentally matched with us in a later round, so it's very helpful.

If you would rather not spectate a round, that's alright. During my BYEs on the Columbia campus, I always worked with my partner on our case based on what we saw our opponent did well. We always saved blocks that we found were helpful and edited our case based on what the opponent poked holes in. But of course, we did this while eating delectable food around. This is the mindset that a winner has — a mindset that isn't too hard on yourself.

Play some Brawl Stars if you will during a BYE, but make sure you get at least a good amount of work done. You're debating for a reason, and you want to place as high as you can.

Another mistake is throwing around random accusations. Throughout my debate career, I've handled these insulting accusations fairly well. In a debate about the federal ban of TikTok, I was called racist when pointing out that China and the United States didn't have the same political views. I don't think I need to go in depth on this because it's honestly common sense, but it is a good thing to know.

Fourthly, it's important to keep your cool. In debate, it's really easy for things to escalate, and the next thing you know, people are yelling. In fact, one of my most shocking memories at a debate tournament is when my opponent got so upset after the round that they lost that she **SLAPPED** her own partner. Just like that!

I noticed that she was generally rude to me as well (she kept laughing during my speech), but I was on the brink of telling her to shut up.

Generally, your opponent is always going to somehow annoy you in some way (unless they're an absolute saint), but it is important to still keep your etiquette when debating and after the round. It honestly builds you a reputation when you compete.

One of our other opponents told us that the girl who slapped her partner got very aggressive during rounds. You don't want to have a poor reputation at a debate league where your opponents **DREAD** debating you. I dread debating the same kids I know who use artificial intelligence or turn bright red when they're yelling at me that I'm just "wrong" without proving it.

Whenever your opponent begins to raise their voice at you or starts cutting you off in crossfire, politely ask if you could continue speaking. Do **NOT** snap back and say, "You interrupted me, can I finish?" The judge knew they interrupted you. You don't need to point it out. The judge will not tolerate the rude behavior and will cut their speaker points. But never lose your own cool, because sometimes opponents can be so sassy that it makes you go silent.

One time this happened to me was during a final round when I was clarifying a misrepresentation my opponent made of my argument. I then asked what they thought of the argument. My opponent plainly said, "I think 'thanks for the clarification.'" I went blank and was kind of stunned. This made me rather quiet for the rest of crossfire because I lost my cool with one sassy remark. Take what your opponent says with a grain of salt and not personally.

I believe a huge casewriting mistake is overloading your arguments. I've seen so many opponents with arguments structured with overarching reasons and then each having three or four subpoints. This is a lot for the judge and the opponent to keep track of. You might be thinking, "But isn't it good for my opponent to be confused?"

No, it's not. This is because you're going to lessen your chances for clash, and the refutations are just going to be an echo chamber of "they misrepresented our argument." This shows the judge you're honestly afraid of actual debate. Anyway, keep your argumentation focused on one aspect of the reason and expand on the further impacts when you weigh.

You're just wasting time for yourself in summary speech and for your opponent. It's also going to make the judge confused about which subpoint holds more weight and what the opponent actually has as a burden. Having several subpoints with several pieces of evidence and several lines of impact is just too much. You're going to end up confusing yourself.

Another casewriting mistake is not using the three rhetorical appeals, which are part of the rhetorical triangle, correctly. The three are **logos, pathos, and ethos**. You might've heard your ELA or Social Studies teacher use these terms before, because these three elements make for a great speech or persuasion.

Logos is exactly what it sounds like — logic. Logos is providing substantial evidence to prove a point, like articles being cited or famous examples in history.

Ethos is making sure that the evidence in the logos part is valid. A study done by an individual with an unknown background in Utah is much more dissuading than a study done by Columbia University. It also answers the question of why we should believe you and your credibility.

Pathos is appealing to emotion. The word "empathy" is kind of in the word. Essentially, to persuade someone, you have to appeal to emotion by appealing to their morals. This is often seen in the impact part of debate, and it makes the listener feel encouraged to do something because you targeted their anger, joy, or sadness.

So what do I essentially mean by not using these three correctly? First, we can dissect the fact that we all know which place each of these rhetorical devices goes when we are writing a case — when we are writing the **AREI** for each contention or argument. Logos is the evidence because that is where we put the substantial proof to try and persuade the judge to go to our side. Ethos is also part of the evidence because citing evidence is very important in order to establish credibility.

This is also used as a small tagline at the end of your case that you make to the judge. You will often hear debaters say, "Thank you, Judge, and I urge you to vote for Affirmative, the side that has the arguments winning on economy."

Lastly is pathos — the emotional appeal. This is often put in the **I** — the impact part of your case. Impacts are usually quite dramatic with the common weighing mechanisms. They're going to make you feel that the judge's decision is very drastic because they might let a scope of people down who are feeling a huge magnitude of weight, whether it be in the short term or the long term.

It is very important that you keep a balance of these three in your speeches because an excess of any might hurt you more than help you. Since I'm a big math fan, I like to remind myself that the rhetorical triangle is equilateral — it's not obtuse or acute. You can come up with whatever reminder you like, but feel free to use mine.

Having too much logos can make your argument sound super strong to you, but in reality, you're not proving to the judge **why** they should care that much. You can throw as many statistics at them as you want, but in the end, it's important to acknowledge that you need to show why it matters — and that's what weighing is all about. You only have so much time in a speech, and filling it up with quotations from universities just wastes it. The judge wants to hear **your** perspective on the evidence, not just an echo chamber for random sources.

Having too much ethos in your debating is just boring. I know there's a good number of debaters out there who get too worked up about sources by calling their opponent out for sources that are from .coms instead of .orgs. I'm going to give you some really shocking news right now: **nobody cares.** Crossfires are the most dry when all you argue about is the validity of a source. The judge is going to end up tuning you out because there's no actual clash happening. Evidence is evidence regardless of the source. Those articles you find online by random news sources still took work to be published and researched. It's just a less extreme level of research than universities do, so don't work yourself up too much.

Having too much pathos is one of the most common overdoses of the rhetorical triangle that I have seen throughout my debate career. The impact will be way too excessive with moral statements like, "Judge, just imagine so many children going through this," and too many individual-based statements. It is important to show the judge how it affects a greater scope of people in a technical way too. For example, it's always great to show how it can affect the economy in the future.

A good impact that I've used in a case would be:

> The impact of this is that the NSA has already stopped 50 potential terrorist attacks from happening, which proves how effective their surveillance is when preventing such attacks. Additionally, these attacks would've been on the stock exchange and, if these attacks were successful, then it would've had a huge effect on our economy. We should be thankful that the NSA stopped these attacks before they were executed and shattered our economy. The information that the NSA has access to does not preserve the names or content of any calls. It only preserves phone numbers. It does not violate the privacy of our citizens. Judge, the safety of our country is always the government's first priority.

Note how this impact didn't just focus on how the NSA's surveillance affects individuals' privacy, but also the impact of NSA surveillance on the entire economy and how the situation the United States is facing is much more serious than just a couple of hurt feelings.

Sometimes, it's hard to tell when an impact has too much pathos because it's just by accident, and that's totally okay. From the same tournament, I have another example impact for a different argument:

> *Judge, the impact of this is that the NSA and our government has been hacked several times and resulted in the theft of over 19 million people's personal data. If it is so easy to hack the government, especially a branch with so much information and power, should we be trusting the NSA with the storing of our private and personal information, oftentimes without our knowledge? The NSA has access to so much of our personal information (even after Congress changed the law to limit what the NSA has access to), and when hackers retrieve this information, hackers can phish, find your Social Security number, ruin your credit, steal money from your bank accounts, and things far worse. Thank you, and we hope you vote for the Affirmative side, the side that cares about the privacy and security of United States citizens and lawful permanent residents.*

This impact had a lot of potential, and I feel that it emphasized too much of the emotional appeal of an individual feeling upset about their privacy being intruded on. Let's edit this impact together.

It's repeated a bunch in this impact that the NSA has access to a lot of information, so let's try to remove that. The sentence "The NSA has access to so much of our personal information (even after Congress changed the law to limit what the NSA has access to) and when hackers retrieve this information, hackers can phish, find your Social Security number, ruin your credit, steal money from your bank accounts, and things far worse" is very basic and only focuses on the individual effects of hacking on a person. While it is important to focus on the individual aspect, let's add the economic aspect of this situation as well.

When hackers hack the government, they will end up retrieving the information of millions of Americans as well as the information of the government, which can allow them to prepare for cyberattacks and potentially things far worse. So now that we know what to remove and what to add, let's write a refined version:

> *Judge, the impact of this is that the NSA and our government has been hacked several times and resulted in the theft of over 19 million people's personal data. The NSA has access to so much of our personal information (even after Congress changed the law to limit what the NSA has access to), and when hackers retrieve this information, hackers can phish, find your Social Security number, ruin your credit, steal money from your bank accounts, and things far worse. In fact, for the economic aspect of this, when hackers retrieve the government's information, it can allow them to prepare for cyberattacks against our government and our citizens, and potentially things far worse. Thank you, and we hope you vote for the Affirmative side, the side that cares about the privacy and security of United States citizens and lawful permanent residents.*

There! That sounds so much better! Let's briefly cover some other minor mistakes:

1) Using too much debate jargon. Many debaters think that this sounds impressive to the judge or intimidates the opponent into losing confidence and losing the debate. This is often not very helpful because most judges are lay judges — some are parent judges who have zero knowledge about debate except for what their child debater told them to get them to judge for the sake of competing. The last thing you want to do is confuse the judge so much that the only things they can understand from the debate are what the opponent interprets of your argument. The opponent will often just misrepresent your argument because that's what refuting is about most of the time — misrepresenting the opponent's argument into something that benefits your side.

2) Casewriting like a blind sheep. What I mean by this is that you essentially write a case that doesn't prepare for blocks/refutations. A lot of people write cases that just blindly prepare for their side while not acknowledging potential refutations that could occur and preparing for them in advance. Preparing for them could look like including evidence or a line of impact from evidence that you've already shown.

An example of this is here:

According to The New York Times, *"The National Security Agency vacuumed up more than 534 million records of phone calls and text messages — more than three times what it collected in 2016. The large and growing volume of data gathered shows that the N.S.A. continues to collect significant amounts of information about Americans' phone and text messages even after changes made by Congress in a law, the USA Freedom Act, which overhauled how the N.S.A. can gain access to domestic telecom data."*

Judge, the impact of this is that the NSA and our government has been hacked several times and resulted in the theft of over 19 million people's personal data. The NSA has access to so much of our personal information (even after Congress changed the law to limit what the NSA has access to), and when hackers retrieve this information, hackers can phish, find your Social Security number, ruin your credit, steal money from your bank accounts, and things far worse. In fact, for the economic aspect of this, when hackers retrieve the government's information, it can allow them to prepare for cyberattacks against our government and our citizens and potentially things far worse. Thank you, and we hope you vote for the Affirmative side, the side that cares about the privacy and security of United States citizens and lawful permanent residents.

This example clearly shows that the person who wrote the argument anticipated a block against them saying that the NSA has access to limited data ever since Congress changed the scope. They replied to this by including a piece of evidence in their argument that states that the NSA still has access to so much information because Congress only removed a small portion of it.

3) Missing framework. A lot of times you'll hear debaters point out to the judge directly that they have a framework of morality, economic benefits, and more.

For example, they might say something like: "The round should be evaluated based on which side better safeguards national security, since the government's primary duty is to protect citizens and security impacts affect the largest number of people most immediately."

So why is having a framework so important? I like to think of your arguments as a building, and the framework is like a portion of the pillars that hold up the building. Your framework essentially holds up your arguments.

4) No internal links between your contentions. Oftentimes, debaters use impact as more of an analysis of the evidence rather than actually demonstrating the impact. While it is important to demonstrate analysis that benefits your side, it is equally important to avoid overloading the judge and to link all of your contentions to the framework.

If you don't understand what I mean, let me simplify it for you.

An example of this is:

- **Reason:** The NSA is a threat to our national security.
- **Evidence:** The NSA holds a lot of information, like phone numbers.
- **Impact:** Our national security is in danger and will affect millions of Americans.

Obviously, this doesn't make sense because the impact did not explain **why** the NSA holding so much information is an impediment to national security. They need to elaborate.

So what did we learn from all of that? We learned the list of mistakes is infinite and that you shouldn't be paranoid about making them, because your case is always going to be flawed in one way or another. My judges tell me to give them more eye contact every single time, even though I increase the amount every single time. Different people like different things, and it's incredibly hard to accustom yourself to all of those preferences.

All I can say is that in debate you need an open mind to make yourself better. I always write down not only the feedback the judge gives me at the end of the round, but also the feedback they give to my opponent, because sometimes I make the same mistakes they do.

If you didn't get a 30 in speaker points in any of your rounds, that's okay. If you didn't get an award in that debate tournament, it's okay. What matters is that you know how to make yourself better, because that can guide you. That's what actually makes you a winner.

11

Beyond Debate

I f I'm going to be completely honest, debate improved me as a person and not only as a student. I know in the past chapters I've been talking a lot about my essays in class being well structured and my presentations being one hundred times better. My academics always meant a lot to me, but I know that this situation is unique and not everyone has the same trifling need for good grades. So why do debate outside of the academic aspects?

I think debate has always been portrayed in the light of a nerdy extracurricular and something that only smart people did "for fun." To be honest, almost every single time I prepared for a debate topic, I didn't know a lot about it and was kind of just daring myself to put myself out on that debate floor and look cool. I always thought that if you knew a lot of things, you were really smart. I didn't know how wrong I was about this statement until the end of 8th grade. I realized that being smart wasn't necessarily knowing a lot, but rather having the knowledge that you *want* to acquire.

There are many reasons why debate isn't just a "nerd" sport like chess or checkers or billiards. (None of those are nerd sports, by the way, but most people often look at them like they are. I love billiards!) Firstly, when you throw yourself out there on the debate floor, it's kind of like performing in theater because sometimes you just have to defend a part that you personally don't believe. *(Disclaimer: debate topics will never be something controversial — my best advice is to leave a debate league immediately if they make controversial topics about religion and more, because that's not going to turn into friendly debate anymore.)* That's not really a nerd thing, is it? People act all the time, and debate kind of helps you do that a little bit more.

Additionally, debate definitely makes you more aware of current events, and that's not something to be looked down upon because some people these days don't understand that most current events affect them directly, even if it isn't quite obvious. I had to do a debate about Article 9 of Japan's constitution, and as a United States citizen, there's no way that could possibly affect me, right?

Wrong!

Japan's usage of Article 9 of their constitution limits their military from settling foreign disputes — foreign disputes that could impact the United States' economy and population. I didn't even know that Japan's Article 9 could mean so much for me, and honestly, that was kind of the thrill of debate. For me, I just got some validation in myself for gaining knowledge, and I know that might sound kind of pathetic, but I promise you, it will make you feel so good and confident in school and just in life.

For starters, I feel like debate made me a more social person. I know I've already spoken about making friends at debate tournaments before, but I think being social expands beyond just making friends at tournaments. I've been friendly with people at high school open houses and on the subway too (life tip: don't be *too* friendly with everyone you meet on the subway). I feel more outspoken at my school events than I was before. I used to just go along and cheer for the people that took part. Soon, I was the person that took part.

Honestly, when I was anticipating my high school orientation, I used to think that I'd be that really awkward, lonely girl in the corner. But I surprised myself — always dragging out icebreakers into something more interesting (no offense to whoever created those icebreakers).

I genuinely tried to make change when I could. I started clubs that I never even thought I could start, which expanded beyond just the familiar faces I saw in the classroom. This was kind of a big step for me because I never really interacted with the kids below the 7th grade. I always thought of them as kind of annoying since they took up most of the space in the hallway and really didn't know how to only stay on one side. I started the Anderson Asian Affinity Group with my best friend, Angela, and made friends across grades. I also started groups catering to my own personal interests, such as a K-pop club.

I also took part in Student Council for two years as a class representative and secretary. I even became closer with my teachers. I feel like I became really close with my debate coach and social studies teacher. He was someone I could talk to if I was experiencing some hardship, and I feel like that's a valuable relationship to have with your teacher because your teacher shouldn't just be your mentor, but also your friend.

This led to me being a sort of mentor myself by launching my website: **freedebateclass.com.** I founded **Civispeak Debate Academy**, an initiative that I started to help teach middle schoolers public forum debate and familiarize them with speaking extemporaneously and analytically. I started giving free debate classes in July of 2025, and I'm continuing to instruct students — right before debate season starts — so students feel confident entering their first official tournament! I even started giving workshops for those who don't want to go in that deep but still immerse themselves in the wonders of debate.

I started this initiative because I believe that all students should have access to the wonderful things that debate can teach. Doing online classes for kids has shown how accessible debate can be for everyone too. This way, they also learn to collaborate with people they might not usually work with if they were at school or in a familiar setting. I also teach with fun drills — not just boring lectures — because it's best to find an approach to learning debate skills without just trying to force them into yourself with words.

Whenever I'm grading the work of kids, I don't think of it as a burden but more as something enjoyable. I enjoy seeing the different perspectives on questions I ask in handouts and trying to figure out how they got to that position. This is really important for me as a teacher to understand because different approaches can help everyone in a class prepare for different situations in debate.

As for confidence, I feel that the practice of speaking in front of people all the time made group projects that I had to present at school more comfortable for me. I used to kind of hate group projects because I liked doing things my way, but I found collaboration to be a critical skill in presenting and building confidence too. One person can't give a presentation all by themselves because they didn't go through the entire process by themselves.

I feel like beyond these basic skills, debate helps you with skills that you don't even realize you're using. Research can actually help you weigh decisions in reality. Often you're going to be faced with a dilemma — whether it be opportunities, drama in your friend group or at school, work in group projects, choosing schools, etc. Research habits make you ask probing questions in real life and further your analysis in real-life situations, whether it be now as a student or later as a member of the workforce.

Additionally, debate can help you emotionally and mentally as well. Debate makes you keep an open mind toward the feedback that the Judge gives you in order to fix your case and your speaking. This is the same kind of open mind you should be keeping when hearing the feedback of others for things such as schoolwork, your other extracurriculars, and just being with friends. Debate also helps you build empathy toward others because since you're keeping an open mind, you essentially have to understand a perspective foreign from your own.

I think one of the biggest things that a lot of people care about is academic performance — and practicing debate does have a positive correlation with academic performance. With debate, you're basically forced to manage a schedule and structure your writing in a perfect manner that is strong and can't easily have holes poked in it by your opponent. This is exactly the kind of dedication you will find yourself putting into essays and just writing in general, and it trains your mind into challenging yourself.

Actually, my math teacher in 8th grade famously advised our class to always "doubt what you know" by essentially asking questions. Yes, the quadratic formula works — but *why* does it work? This promotes deeper analysis and thinking on a road to better understanding, which is what all students want to achieve.

I know a lot of parents and students are concerned about high school and college applications, and debate can work as an asset for you. Essentially, this proves to colleges that you have a diverse array of skills that would benefit not only you but their campus as well. They want to see that you made a modest difference for yourself. Remember how I spoke about being more outspoken and generally more thrilled in learning? I had built a community for myself out of nothing but a little interest. That's the kind of change that colleges love to see in kids.

Additionally, structuring arguments and learning how to talk with formality is generally beneficial for writing those college essays and interviews. Debating is all about being able to respectfully disagree with your opponent and give more to your answers to clash points than just one-liners, and that's the kind of analysis that Judges like to see a lot — and it can help you win many rounds.

Because of debate, I feel that I have become a great writer and wrote this book at the age of fourteen. I was able to build the confidence to not only read aloud my writing in seminars in class or in that debate room, but put it out there for the public, which is not something I would've immediately agreed to a couple of years ago. I used to be timid with my writing abilities — fearing that I sounded old or just like a copy of a book I recently read. But I was able to curate my own voice, and this is something I believe *anyone* can do with the right motivation.

12

Beginning for Yourself

S o now that I've spent so much time talking about debate, how it's intriguing in itself, and how it's also just a great extracurricular with a long list of benefits, how do you actually get started?

A lot of schools offer a debate club or debate team, which you should totally join to get started! If you're part of a club — a debate group that just practices amongst themselves — then you should take initiative in the club to enroll your club into a debate league and create a team. There will be a fee that varies in amount depending on the league, but it's always best to try.

Some schools have debate teams that are on a tryout basis, and I know it can probably be pretty scary to try out. All of the teams that I have been on were not on a tryout basis, but I know some friends from debate who did have a situation like that. If you have to try out by writing an argumentative speech on a topic and giving it, or doing extemporaneous speaking, don't fret! Follow the exercises that I mentioned in the 9th chapter. These will allow you to mentally prepare yourself for the tryout and prove to your coach that you are putting in an effort to immerse yourself in the world of debate — whether or not they take that away from you. This kind of motivation is something that debate coaches really like to see and often practice during their team practices.

I remember my team practices were really laid back, and we were allowed to just work on our cases with our teams or gather a group of us to play those debate card games or exercises. We enjoyed these card games so much that sometimes, when there was a substitute teacher, we would take the card games and play them once we finished our work (this is a devious trick that I don't think our debate coach/social studies teacher ever found out).

Team practices were one of my favorite parts of being on the debate team because I got to hang out with a bunch of upperclassmen and lowerclassmen. I always got comments from my opponents that my debate coaches were the most chill and coolest debate coaches they had ever met, and I'm always really proud of the fact that my coach's method of being laid back really worked for not only me, but for everyone on the team. The Anderson School's debate team was kind of known for being one of the best in every league that we competed in.

If you don't have such a large group of people to call a club or team, then you and another person can enroll in a league as a unit. This will also cost a fee. They might make you join under the tournament's personal team filled with other units who didn't have a large team. But don't be scared to do this, because this is always a chance to meet new people and make new friends. It's like enrolling into a swim team or other outside-of-school sports teams.

If you don't have a partner to join a league with, then that's totally okay! How exactly do you find a partner for you? Don't focus too much on trying to find a partner who's great at public speaking or really smart in class. Just find someone who has the spirit of debate, because eventually, you guys will learn the dynamics of debate together!

One of the best ways to find a partner is just looking through communities you're already a part of. If you're part of a sports team, ask someone. If you're not home-schooled, ask someone at school. If you're part of a community service, ask someone. If you can't find anyone that's available, then that's okay. Email a league describing your interest in participating in their program but not having a partner. Likely, other kids will be emailing them with similar situations, so they might pair you up with someone. But it's always best to do what your parent or guardian is most comfortable with, as they might be hesitant to email leagues in such situations.

Don't hesitate to even ask people you never thought you would find yourself working with. It can always be the start of a new friendship.

The girl I partnered with for my very first tournament wasn't a close friend of mine at all, but we built a wonderful friendship just from all the hours we spent working with each other. The two boys I partnered with for the championship tournament in 8th grade were just classmates of mine, and we became the ultimate trio!

If you do find a partner but you can't exactly find a league that hosts tournaments in an area that you're comfortable traveling to for debate, then there are some other approaches you can have. Thanks to technology, some debate tournaments are hosted online, and it's really accessible to do from home. There aren't many debate leagues that do this consistently except during the winter months. If you do want the full debate experience, I still recommend going to in-person debates. It's really fun and allows a lot more bonding with teammates, opponents, coaches, and more. In fact, me and my friends would always go to the Columbia University vending machines for gummy bears at every tournament hosted there. You can have similar traditions with your team to keep up with the fun!

I think that debate is generally something that's easy for anyone to start because it's practically made for anyone with any kind of schedule. Tournaments by a league are usually only once per month, starting from October or November and lasting until April or May. But I do suggest not jumping into debate immediately every season, especially if you have an important standardized test coming up. I personally think you shouldn't cancel going to a debate tournament just because you have a few tests in school coming up, because that's all a part of balancing workloads in all aspects of your life.

If you're part of another team that has overlapping tournaments, don't fret. In my opinion, you should see what level you're at for each respective extracurricular and decide which one needs you the most at that moment. I've had debate tournaments that had overlapping events, and I ended up just choosing the tournament that I felt like I would have a better time being at. I often chose the tournament where the judges were better and the Tabroom situation was better, and making my decision based off of that almost always led to me feeling content.

I know many people say that you debate all the time, and that is true. Debate doesn't have to be formal. I know all of you have had disagreements, but during your disagreements, you probably didn't use "Well, I'm just right because I am right!" as your main justification. You probably reasoned yourself through it, and then when you and the "disagreer" both gave your reasons, you probably said that they weren't right because of something else — a different factor. This should sound a lot like debate! Debate doesn't always have to be so hostile, either. In classrooms, they started promoting debate because it's good to learn the skill of respectfully disagreeing with someone and keeping an open mindset to others' opinions. It's fun to listen to others too, so don't get so ahead of yourself with the speaking that you shut down your opponent, because it often makes the debate less clashy.

All in all, I encourage you to have fun in your debate career. Don't feel pressured to have amazing placings every time and instead create goals that rise at a small level. Usually, I beat myself up over bad test scores and my overall grade going down by a percent, but debate really humbled me. I realized I couldn't be the best at everything and it navigated me through the process of understanding how to create goals that weren't too far-fetched. Creating these realistic goals helped keep both my academics and debate skills in good condition!

You've probably done this before too and haven't realized it. You might've gotten an 80 on a test, and then when you worked a little harder the next time, you got an 87. Then you slowly increased your grade goals to something that you preferred over an 90 and still made you and your parents content.

Additionally, don't discourage yourself in debate when your opponent laughs or snickers while you're giving a speech or talking. The judge will probably notice and, if not, it's probably going to bite them back later. Trust me!

Even though I've only competed at 23 tournaments and have gotten 30 awards in middle school, the awards are just keepsakes of time. The real treasure I have found from debate is the confidence, public speaking, and leadership skills I have retained. I hope you can see the same for yourself — there's only one way to find out: by competing! You might not find these immediately, but trust the amount of time it takes to find these treasures.

IV

Part Four

In this chapter, I help you plan out your first case-writing by giving you a mock resolution (or you could use one that you're preparing for) and go through all the steps of a day-to-day schedule of casewriting. Exercises start from the brainstorming stage and end with nice weighing exercises to incorporate during the round (being prepared is always great!).

13

Guided Written Exercises

I n previous chapters, I've provided a lot of vocal and mental exercises to help train you for the spontaneity of debate and extemporaneous speaking. In this chapter, I'm going to give you a lot of exercises to help you train your casewriting skills and block writing skills because these are equally as important as the speaking that you do during the round.

Let's start with the root of casewriting: argument brainstorming. A sample topic that we're going to be using throughout all the exercises described in this chapter is one of my favorite ones that I have debated: **Resolved: New York City should enact congestion pricing for all major parts of Manhattan.** This is just a sample resolution, so feel free to use any resolution you're interested in preparing for — like one you have a debate tournament upcoming for or one you're genuinely interested in. The vagueness of this resolution allows for a lot of clash points to be brought up during the round.

Let's start with brainstorming some arguments. When brainstorming arguments, I like to think of arguments based on the knowledge that I already have and put them in a table. Just put the arguments out there so you can start feeling comfortable.

Affirmative	Negative
Reason 1:	Reason 1:
Reason 2:	Reason 2:
Reason 3:	Reason 3:
Reason 4:	Reason 4:
Reason 5:	Reason 5:

If you have more than five reasons for each side, go ahead and fill them in. Now initiate some research on the reasons that you found based on my research tips that I described in the chapter on casewriting (Chapter 5).

Now, let's fill out a second table.

In this handout, you would have chosen your final three reasons based on the ones you found were the most substantial during your research. For these three reasons for each respective side, you're going to find three pieces of evidence that support each reason. In your finalized speech, you're probably not going to use all three because of the lack of time, but we want to have a plethora of evidence to choose from when we make our final decision, so we also have extra evidence pieces for other arguments because you never know what use some piece of evidence will be!

Affirmative

Reason	Evidence
	1) 2) 3)
	1) 2) 3)
	1) 2) 3)

Negative

Reason	Evidence
	1) 2) 3)
	1) 2) 3)
	1) 2) 3)

When you fill out the table above, star the piece of evidence that you find the most beneficial after a few minutes of just contemplating and looking at the array of things that you found. Remember to look back at the tips I provided for good evidence pieces in Chapter 5. Remember to shorten your evidence piece effectively so you're not wasting time saying sentences about things irrelevant to the argument at hand! Now, let's move to the third exercise.

In the third exercise, we're going to be moving onto the last part of the AREI structure — the **impact**. Now that we have our three reasons for each side and a piece of evidence (or two) for each of them, we need to contemplate what the Judge should be taking into account for each argument and set up the weighing for the future. When we're thinking of writing an impact, remember to think of how many people could potentially be affected by the argument, how severe it is, whether or not the negative outcomes are reversible, and more. Let's fill in the table! If you need more space, feel free to work in the margins or copy down this table onto another paper.

Affirmative

Reason	Evidence	Impact

Negative

Reason	Evidence	Impact

Now that we finished the draft for each case, we need to think about the grand scheme of the **arguments**. We need to choose which arguments are the most important and label the arguments in such an order that the most important argument with the biggest impact we would like to point out to the Judge goes first. We want to ensure we have enough time to get our most important argument out there. Take a few minutes to write numbers down to each argument and decide!

Let's work on the next piece of important business — **BLOCKS!**

Block writing is one of my favorite parts of preparing for a debate because I just love telling people why they're wrong (don't take it personally!). There are so many arguments out there, but you need to decide which ones are the ones you want to write blocks to because you obviously don't have all the time in the world.

First, we're going to start by writing blocks to our OWN arguments — even the ones that we scrapped when argument brainstorming because it's likely that one of our opponents will have them if they're common to think of. We have to understand that when writing blocks, we're not trying to write refutations to the evidence that we prepared but to the overall argument, because the chances of our opponent having the exact same evidence that we had is pretty slim, so we need to broaden our minds when preparing. But remember to have evidence that backs up your refutation because Judges love when you not only structure your cases but your clash points. Fill in the table below using this advice.

Affirmative

Argument Reason	Refutation

Negative

Argument Reason	Refutation

If you have block ideas to arguments that you didn't brainstorm or use for yourself, feel free to write them down! The more prepared you are, the better! The table above is just for you to practice writing blocks and get into the habit of doing that before a tournament.

When writing the blocks, you probably looked at your arguments and thought that they probably needed tweaking. That's why what we came up with before was just the first draft! Now we can edit our cases accordingly to the potential holes our opponent can poke.

Now we're going to rewrite each case, but in the bulleted format of AREI so it's clearer to read, in the order that we want the arguments to be in, and with any final edits made.

AFFIRMATIVE:

A:

R:

E:

I:

A:

R:

E:

I:

A:

R:

E:

I:

NEGATIVE

A:

R:

E:

I:

A:

R:

E:

I:

A:

R:

E:

I:

Now that we have a copy of each case that we would be ready to go into a tournament with and a nice set of blocks to use, we can now prepare a summary speech.

When writing a summary speech, we want to create an outline for ourselves. When we do this, we want to reflect on all the burdens the person giving a summary speech needs to cover, referred to in Chapter 7. Write down your outline with fill-in-the-blanks for your summary speech in the space below.

_____

_____

_____

_____

_____

_____

_____

_____

_____

_____

_____

_____

_____

_____

_____

_____

_____

_____

_____

_____

_____

_____

_____

_____

_____

_____

_____

_____

_____

_____

_____

_____

_____

_____.

Now you might be thinking we're probably going to be drafting a final focus now. **Wrong!** Final focuses should basically be plainly about what happened in the round, and you can't prewrite them. But we can practice elements of them — like **weighing**!

This exercise will help you with common weighing situations you'll come across in debate, like morals, economics, individual rights, etc. Below, for each question, you will be given two options, and you will have to prove why each outweighs the other (individually).

For example, if the question was "climate change vs poverty," I would have to write in two different sections. In the first section, I would write how climate change outweighs poverty. In the second section, I would write vice versa. When doing this, remember to use the weighing mechanisms that we spoke about. Feel free to expand from the common five weighing mechanisms and branch out to other ones! **This** is an exercise, and you should feel comfortable trying new **mechanisms** that you want to use in real rounds later on.

1) CLIMATE CHANGE vs POVERTY

Climate change outweighs poverty on _____

_____

Poverty outweighs climate change on _____

_____

2) PRIVACY vs SAFETY

Privacy outweighs safety on _____

_____

Safety outweighs privacy on _____

_____

3) LONG TERM SOLUTION WITH WAITING vs EFFICIENT SHORT TERM SOLUTION

A long term solution that requires waiting outweighs an efficient short term solution _____

_____

_____

_____

_____

_____

_____

_____

_____

_____

_____

_____

An efficient short term solution outweighs a long term solution that requires waiting _____

_____

_____

_____

_____

_____

_____

_____

_____

_____

_____

4) DATA BREACH vs ECONOMY

A data breach outweighs economic detriments/benefits _____

_____

Economic detriments/benefits outweigh a data breach _____

_____

Some of these were a little hard to do for both sides, and that was intentional, because you never know what side you'll end up playing in the actual tournament, and you need to find a way out of a sticky situation. Now that we have had some practice weighing, we're prepared for a major part of final focus. The other part of final focus is condensing the round to a few clash points. We've already really covered the way to do this in Chapter 8.

About the Author

Bani Kaur Rawal is a Student Champion and Debate Instructor from New York City who first discovered debate in middle school—and never looked back. What began as a single after-school activity quickly grew into a passion for critical thinking, persuasive speaking, and leadership.

Bani went on to compete at tournaments, win awards, and teach debate online to students across the country. She attended The Anderson School and now studies at The Spence School, where she continues to share her commitment to youth empowerment and public speaking.

As the founder of **Civispeak Debate Academy**, Bani has coached young speakers to find their voice, express themselves boldly, and lead with confidence inside and outside the round. She believes that every student—regardless of background, experience, or stage fright—can learn to debate like a champion